NON-SEXIST CHILDRAISING

CARRIE CARMICHAEL

non-sexist

childraising

BEACON PRESS · BOSTON

Beacon Press books are published under the auspices
of the Unitarian Universalist Association
Published simultaneously in Canada by
Fitzhenry & Whiteside Limited, Toronto

(hardcover) 9 8 7 6 5 4 3 2 1
(paperback) 9 8 7 6 5 4 3 2

Grateful acknowledgment is made to Action for Children's
Television for permission to reprint the text of their
"Treat TV with T.L.C." poster.

Library of Congress Cataloging in Publication Data

Carmichael, Carrie.
  Non-sexist childraising.
  Bibliography: p.
    1. Children—Management.   2. Sexism—United States.
3. Femihism—United States.   4. Sex differences
(Psychology).   I. Title.
HQ769.C339   649'.1   76–48497
ISBN 0-8070-2738-3
ISBN 0-8070-2739-1

For Casey Carmichael Greenfield
and the children she may have

91830

ACKNOWLEDGMENTS

It was MaryAnn Lash, Associate Director of Beacon Press, who suggested that "But What About Our Sons?" an article Lindsy Van Gelder and I wrote for the October 1975 issue of *Ms.* magazine might be the beginning of a book. I thank her for her initial and continued interest in how feminists are raising their children. She encouraged me to look at the changing relationships within feminist families, and not confine myself to mothers and sons, or mothers and daughters. She has been a support, an intelligent guide, and a comfort. I am grateful, since because of MaryAnn Lash and this book, I've been able to do research for my own non-sexist parenting.

My appreciation to Charlotte Cecil Raymond of Beacon Press for her judgment and her enthusiasm.

I offer loving appreciation to my daughter Casey Carmichael Greenfield for being. Also, for her cooperation, patience, and encouragement as she watched me disappear to "write on the book about children."

To my husband, Jeff Greenfield, I extend the grown-up version of my thanks to our daughter. He had confidence in me, love for me, and played Participatory-Papa-*Par-Excellence.*

I thank Lindsy Van Gelder for working with me on the "Sons" piece for *Ms.,* for her teaching and for her years of friendship.

I am grateful to James W. Walkup, Jr., for his integral part in the evolutionary process.

Mary Elizabeth Daly provided magical experiences weekly for Casey as I worked on this book and provided friendship and intellectual challenge for me. Thank you.

Paige Massman and Maria Neuwirth, as friends and neighbors, gave me valuable support both intangible and tangible. They offered the kind of assistance every working parent needs — loving care for my child.

I thank Rosemarie Schieffer for her help with the typing.

I am grateful to Harriet Wentlandt Carmichael and William Carmichael for setting me on the road to feminism. Helen Greenwald Greenfield and Benjamin Greenfield generously gave familial love to one who married in, and relieved a working mother with grandmothering.

I owe the most thanks and appreciation to the parents, professionals, and children who openly shared themselves with me. They alternately made me excited, sad, furious, jealous, and thrilled. They told me and, more importantly, showed me that it is possible to live a non-sexist life.

CONTENTS

INTRODUCTION

In the last ten years the women's movement has raised the consciousness of the nation. Laws have been changed, the language has been altered, and old habits have been challenged. Parents who believe in the equality of the sexes are breaking important new ground in the method of childraising. Alone or in small groups, these feminist mothers and fathers are working to develop techniques to raise children into fair-minded, non-sexist adults. These parents are devising a grid through which their children will view an unfair world and be able to screen out sexism. There is no textbook for these pioneer parents, and their own children are in a sense the experimental animals.

Essentially this book is a report on how the project of rearing non-sexist children is going. An attempt to build a bridge between feminists working in isolation, it is a clearinghouse of ideas of what is being done and what still can be done to combat sexism. There are no foolproof formulae offered, no alphabet of rules to follow. There is a sharing of ideas, suggestions, and experiences.

My sources are parents and feminist families all over the country who are trying to de-program the male-dominated society we live in. They shared with me the techniques they are using, their successes, their theories. My sources are the children. Do these kids today think differently? Are even relatively non-sexist children considered freaks? Do they see themselves as a generation of pioneers?

My sources are the psychologists, psychiatrists, pediatricians, and educators who deal with these frontier families.

Many professionals that I interviewed offered their personal opinions and experiences as well. Data from their lives as parents, and the combination of professional theory and practice, merged in these feminist thinkers to create some reasonable, workable non-sexist techniques.

I spoke with whites and blacks and browns. My sources have diverse lifestyles, running the gamut from persons living on public assistance, to coupon clippers living off trust funds. My interview subjects are from a variety of ethnic, educational, and economic backgrounds.

I found the guidance counselor in Massachusetts who shares a common goal with the housewife in Chicago. I talked with the retailer in New Jersey and the psychologist in Washington State who are battling the same frustrations. I listened to the librarian in California and the physician in the District of Columbia who have both cried "uncle" in the sexism struggle.

The lives of some of my sources have been revolutionized by the women's movement. Others have abandoned the idea of revolution for themselves but retain the hope that life will be fairer for their children.

No national organization for non-sexist childraising is listed in the telephone directory — yet. No agent offers non-sexist parents and children for interview. There are no press releases on the subject, no established nationwide network to plug into — I hope that is one thing this book promotes. My search was a grassroots approach. Feminist groups, both formal and informal, are passionately interested in the issue of childraising. As a result, my sources multiplied in a geometric progression. Quasi-feminists and even sexists were willing to talk. Everyone, I was not really surprised to discover, has an opinion on how to raise children — even persons with no present relationship with children. Everyone feels she or he has *the* credential to advise on childrearing. For everyone, save Athena, did start out life as a child.

NON-SEXIST CHILDRAISING

WHAT IS NON-SEXIST CHILDRAISING?

FOR years the message from the women's movement was that Motherhood was a bum rap — a crummy job, thankless and scorned. Those of us who wanted to be both feminists and mothers received little, if any, support from our sisters. Children, we were told, were to be aborted, shoved into day care, or given to their fathers. Children symbolized oppression incarnate. More energy was expended figuring out ways to get rid of them than examining how to raise them.

Fortunately the passage of time has mellowed this cry. The angry feminist of 1969 who perhaps swore off men and children, and most certainly swore at them, has discovered she can have both in her life and still be a feminist. She can offer her children a very different kind of upbringing from the type she had. She can do non-sexist childraising.

Just what is non-sexist childraising? The term *sexist* was coined as a parallel to *racist* to mean "prejudiced by a person's gender." *Sexist* is, to my mind, an awkward, convoluted sounding, Latinate word. *Non-sexist* is worse; it is negative, hyphenated, and means "against gender prejudice, against unfair treatment for males and females because of their sex."

A more positive label for the kind of childraising today's feminists are practicing would be something like "open-options childraising," or "free/fair-minded childraising." Or, like the *Ms.* magazine project that is a book, record, and television special, "Free to Be You and Me"-childraising. Calling products of this kind of childraising Free Children is about the best term so far. But it still is not exact enough.

Parents raising non-sexist children are against pervasive gender prejudice, but what are they for? Are they for dresses on boys? Destruction of the nuclear family? Raising girls and boys to be exactly alike? Some people think so.

Over and over again during the course of this project I've been asked, "Just what is this non-sexual childraising?" — as if it involved raising children without genitals. Adults with children and some without repeatedly asked, "Do you think you can raise a non-sexist child? Is it a good idea to try and make boys and girls the same?" The questioners have misunderstood.

Assumptions about just what non-sexist childraising means are sometimes grossly erroneous. Part of the confusion is a function of the vocabulary. There are gradations of misinformation about what non-sexist childraising is. One extreme is the image of parents forcing all children into sameness. Hup, two — all children into overalls, T-shirts, shoes of identical cut and color. This extreme denies sex differences. Children are told merely that they are children, not girls and boys. Non-sexist, in this view, means no sex, an enforced androgyny. The other end of the spectrum for defining non-sexist childraising is to give a boy a doll, a girl a truck, and call their upbringing non-sexist. The project is much more complicated than that.

Raising a child free of gender prejudice has as its goal celebrating the myriad differences among girls and girls, and boys and boys — not blunting the differences between girls and boys. It is freeing the child to be whomever or whatever he or she wants to be, not squelching the variations because they do not conform to some arbitrary definition of what a man is, or what a woman is. It is freeing the personalities and helping children to develop the strength to sustain their own differentness in the face of adversity.

Encouraging children to define themselves according to personality instead of sex frightens people. Voices tinged with fear have asked me, "There are differences between boys and girls, aren't there?" Of course there are — one sex has one set of equipment, one sex has another set. But genital and chromosomal build is the only way every boy is different from every girl.

The goal of parents raising non-sexist children is to nurture offspring who can make their own choices about their lives — choices that are not limited because of a child's sex. This goal is simple enough — realizing it is not.

What makes up non-sexist childraising? It requires a commitment to create an open, fair environment for a child. This often means the parents must take a long hard look at their own sexism, their own assumptions of what is mothering and what is fathering, and examine how they relate to each other. It most certainly means not doing what comes naturally, but sometimes adopting a rigid pattern of parental duties to avoid falling into the stereotype.

Non-sexist childraising means telling and showing a child she or he can, as one feminist mother told me, "Make his life a work of art."

Non-sexist childraising means helping a child create a grid through which to view a sexist world. It means paying ceaseless attention to the details of deprogramming everything that bombards a child and tells her/him how to be. To some parents non-sexist childraising means not only deprogramming, but severely screening out sexist input.

It means educating children about the women's movement, the history of female oppression and male oppression, too.

It means providing a child with a world full of options in the form of toys, books, learning materials. It means working within the family and in the schools and other institutions for active sexual equality.

Non-sexist childraising is an everyday job.

Who raises non-sexist children? Why, feminist families, a breed that comes in all different shapes and sizes. They don't belong to a national organization, and often they are isolated from one another.

A feminist family is one that believes in equality of the sexes — but more than paying lip service to an ideal while living according to the dictates of a sexist world, this family makes its sexual politics personal. Every day a feminist family fights against the society that loudly and clearly, as well as subliminally, tells females and males what they are supposed to do. Daily a feminist family battles the set of do's and don'ts they were brought up with.

Who are the feminist families? Ones that define themselves so.

They are Joan and Penny who live with their daughters. There are no men in their lives and militant feminist posters decorate their walls.

They are Louise and Tom and their two daughters. Louise wants a non-sexist life for her children, but lives a stereotyped life with Tom. She's a feminist living with a male chauvinist.

A feminist family is Ken and his boy and girl. His consciousness was raised when his wife left.

A separated feminist family is Paula and Tom and son William. Half the week William lives with his mother, half the week with his father.

Another feminist family is Laura and her two daughters. Ben has custody of the girls every other weekend.

There are Barbara and John who live in a big house with their girl and boy and sundry grownups and children and animals.

There are Mike and Lynn who have decided against breastfeeding their baby because it is something they can't share.

There are Bob and Michelle who live a stereotyped life (he works, she stays home with the kids), but both are feminist thinkers. They expose their kids to other lifestyles, showing them a non-sexist way.

There are more.

What these families share is a vision for the equality of the sexes. They have taken it upon themselves — sometimes together and other times, as in the case of Louise, alone — to fight for a fairer life for their children.

How do you raise your children? Are you raising them the way you were raised, doing what comes naturally? If so, it probably means a fairly rigid sex role differentiation.

See for yourself. Answer the following questionnaire about the breakdown of tasks within your home and for the care of your children. (Single parents, take a look at all the jobs you perform alone.)

> Who stays home when the kids are sick?
> Who calls the sitter?
> Whose name is called when a nightmare rips through a child's sleep?
> Who deals with the school and teachers?
> Who shops for the food?
> Who prepares the meals?
> Who does the cleaning?
> Who neatens?
> Who does the laundry?
> Who shops for the children's clothes?
> Which parent is called when a child is hurt?
> Who soothes and snuggles the kids?
> Who dresses the kids?
> Who changes the diapers?
> Who gets up in the night for a feeding?
> Who takes the kids to school?
> Who takes the kids to the doctor? dentist?
> Who decides where to go on vacations?
> Who doles out the weekly allowance?
> Who disciplines?
> Who decides how money's to be spent?
> Who supports the family?

How do your answers come out? Quite evenly divided between "Mamas" and "Papas," with a lot of "Both Mama and Papa" answers? If so, even if you don't know it, you are practicing a degree of non-sexist parenting. The children in your life are learning by your example that the ability to fold undershirts is not chromosomally determined. From that, your children can begin to extrapolate that little else is.

If your scorecard reads almost exclusively "Mama," with "Papa" taking only the last four or five questions, then your parenting is of the sexist variety, regardless of the liberal

books on your shelves, or the feminist magazines you sub-
scribe to. It's possible to go braless and still be a sexist mother.
Sexual politics is personal politics. Declamations about equal
rights for both sexes and support for the Equal Rights
Amendment on the outside matters very little if children and
parents live a sexist life inside. Children do as we demonstrate, not as we demonstrate for.

What follows are two exaggerated days — one stretched on
the side of oppression and stereotype, the other exaggerated
in the direction of perfection. Where are you in comparison
to the two?

2

A DAY IN THE LIFE

As Jean Meyer heard Tom's key turn in the lock, she read 5:45 on the clock. She was exhausted. The day with Kevin, five, and sixteen-month-old Dara had begun almost twelve hours before with tears and cries for "milk" and "Mommy." Jean dimly remembered stumbling out from under the quilt covering a sleeping Tom, and rushing to soothe Dara in another room.

She wanted to comfort Dara, but most of all she wanted Dara to be quiet. "Sssh, sssh, lovey, your brother is still sleeping. Sssh, Daddy is sleeping. Let me change your diaper. You'll be more comfortable when you are dry."

God forbid, she should wake up Kevin at this hour. He might wake up cheery now, but he'd make her life miserable after school. If Tom was disturbed, he'd make her life miserable now. He wants to sleep in the mornings, and she wants not to be yelled at. "Can't you keep those kids quiet?" he had barked the last time. That was at 6:30 A.M. He'd be surlier at 6.

This morning Jean succeeded. Dara didn't wake her father up. The alarm clock at 7:15 did and when Jean heard the rush of Tom's shower water, she relaxed. There'd be no scene this morning. Jean set the breakfast table, then gently roused Kevin and helped him dress for kindergarten. Tom dressed himself as little Dara examined the used pipe cleaners in her father's ashtray. When she started to put them in her mouth, Tom yelled to Jean in the other room. "Jean, Dara's putting something in her mouth."

He was finishing the knot in his rep tie as Jean careened

through the doorway, gouged her hip on the dresser, then deftly removed the pipe cleaners and ashtray in one motion. "Dirty — don't put things in your mouth, Dara." She peered at her daughter with concern, then relief. No harm. She'd gotten there in time. "Tom," she said, trying very hard to be civil, "you saw her put the pipe cleaners in her mouth. If you had time to yell for me, you had time to walk over and stop her." "I am getting dressed for *work*," he said defensively and proudly. Jean felt her stomach slide the way it did whenever they talked about making money, or rather, his making money and her not. She felt guilty — guilty that he had the burden to support the family now. Tom worked hard at the office and needed rest at home. Jean worked hard before he went to the office, while he was there, and after he got back. She got little rest at home.

Tom was getting dressed. He couldn't do two things at one time, even if one thing was saving his daughter from harm. "You didn't clean that ashtray last night, Jean. That's why she's into it." Jean felt herself starting to scream, but she choked it off. What was the use? They'd been through this same fight so many times. *His* ashes and pipe cleaners in *his* ashtray on the night table on *his* side of the bed were her responsibility to clean up. That's how he saw it. She couldn't convince him otherwise. Carrying Dara in one arm and Kevin's school clothes in the other, Jean walked down to the kitchen with Kevin at her side.

Even the napkins were in place when the four of them sat down for breakfast. But immediately an unpleasant smell of toddler diarrhea cut through the aroma of coffee and toasted English. Jean scooped up the smelly baby and toted her back to her room for a clean diaper and clean overalls. Buttoning the straps, Jean anticipated a day of diarrhea and at least one wash load of smelly stained laundry.

Dara made her own way back to the kitchen table while Jean rinsed the soiled pajamas, and carefully washed her hands free of diarrhea and ointment. Jean was hungry. So was Dara, and she strained to climb into her high chair while her father and brother finished their eggs. Dara didn't mind that all her food and drink had reached the same temperature. Jean would have preferred a steaming egg and a less stiff English muffin, but she couldn't see starting all over again. She hadn't the energy and didn't want to waste the already-prepared food. Consoling herself with a promise that after the males went off to work and school, she'd have a really good, hot cup of coffee, she ate the egg and muffin. She needed the protein; there was a long day ahead.

Finishing his second cup of coffee, Tom got up from the table, and slipped on his blue gabardine blazer. Leaving his dishes at his place, he made his way around the breakfast table to say good-bye to his family. He tousled Kevin's hair and playfully punched the boy's shoulder. "Have a good day at school, kid. Don't give the teacher too much trouble." Kevin pushed the hair out of his eyes and grinned back at his dad. Tom patted Dara ever so softly on her hair, steering clear of the visible egg yolk on her face and fingers, and the invisible, but imminent, diarrhea. As she sat in her chair, Jean was kissed on the cheek by a Tom who held his body as far away as possible from threat of stain or smell.

Saying "Good-bye," Tom walked out the door. Both adults breathed sighs of relief. Sure, I'm glad we had the kids, thought Tom, but I wish you could pack them in plastic wrap and bring them out when they are about eighteen. I'm not an anal compulsive, nothing like that. I'm not *that* clean, but God, kids are *so* messy! Moments later and miles away, an elevator took Tom into his world of chrome and glass and rosewood veneer.

Jean was left in her world of diapers and dishes, but when Tom was away she didn't feel nearly as angry and resentful as she did when he was home. With Kevin gone, Jean began her morning routine — table to clear, dishes to do, dinner to consider. Did she have something in the freezer for tonight? She only needed two lamb chops for the kids; the grown-ups were going out.

Once Kevin's bed was made, she moved along to Dara's room. I'm so glad I had a girl, she thought looking at Dara. In a couple of years I'll have somebody to help me in the house.

As young as she was, Dara was beginning to help. "Thank you, Dara," Jean called as the little girl dropped her father's socks and underpants into the hamper. Jean had never thought of asking Kevin to help when he was Dara's age. And now, you just couldn't get that boy to put his clothes in the hamper, or even hang them up most of the time. And making his bed, Ha! She'd tried that too. Why, Kevin was just like his father. Men!

Jean collected the dirty laundry and headed toward the laundry room. I'd rather do this hefting and sorting of soiled laundry before I shower, rather than after, she decided. Imitating her mother, and being encouraged to do so, Dara stretched up on tiptoe to throw undershirts into the washing machine.

At 9:45 Jean clicked on the television set, turned to "Sesame Street," and peeled off her bathrobe. In the fifteen minutes left to the program, she figured she could shower her body, shampoo her hair and shave her legs and underarms. It was a race against the clock. All the while she listened through the suds and shower for Dara. The house was childproofed, but there was always the threat of something happening to a sixteen-month-old. Jean always left the bathroom door slightly ajar when she showered. Dara couldn't turn knobs yet, so a closed door was the same as a locked door to her. Today, like so many other times, Dara toddled into the bathroom, opening wide the door and bringing in a blast of cold air. "Mama?" "Dara?" Mama?" as if to say, "just checking."

When Kevin came home from school, Jean fixed him a lunch of soup, peanut-butter sandwiches, milk, and the ever-present apple juice. Spills, crumbs, and dishes, combined with requests for things not in the cupboard, made this Tuesday lunch not very different from any other. At lunch Kevin often talked about what went on in the kindergarten classroom, or on the playground. How the boys played "Star Trek" and shot each other with space guns. How Donny Werby cried like a sissy when he was downed by a space gun and scraped his knee. "How the other boys laughed! He cried just like a girl." This kind of story upset Jean, but she was never quite sure why. Just the way boys are, she thought. But it was strangely disturbing that five-year-old Kevin, who himself sobbed in the night about the monsters in his dreams and cried real tears when he was hurt badly, ridiculed another child for crying.

When Jean heard Tom's key in the lock, she quickly combed her hair. Tom was not really glad to be home, but he was relieved and glad not to be at the office any more. Tired from a full day on the phone, at a meeting, at the dictaphone, he was eager to take off his tie and relax. After putting down his briefcase, he walked into the kitchen to greet his family. Again, he did not get too close. Sometimes he kissed the baby, but not tonight. Cooked carrot had worked its way into her hair. Fearing damage to his jacket, Tom decided he'd kiss the baby later. He clapped his son on the back. Jean got a kiss. She smelled of lamb chop.

Leaving the family in the kitchen, Tom took off his coat and walked into the bedroom, drink in his hand. He'd relax a bit, read the afternoon paper, watch the news before showering and dressing to go out to dinner. Tom was exhausted and needed some peace and quiet. Jean better keep the kids out of his hair and out of earshot.

Dinner for the kids over, Jean cleaned the pots, washed the dishes and made sure the kitchen counters were crumbless, before she ran the bath water for Dara. Kevin could bathe himself at his age. He created puddles on the bathroom floor and always left two or more towels in wet, soggy piles on the tile, just like his father.

Jean kept her eye on the clock. 6:30 P.M. That gave her an hour before the babysitter arrived. An hour to bathe Dara and get her into a double thick diaper so she wouldn't wake up in the middle of the night crying because she was wet and cold and uncomfortable. An hour to supervise Kevin's night-time routine — bath, nightclothes, teeth brushing and fluoride rinse — and let him play with his father before Tom had to dress for going out. Would there be time for it all? Jean always perspired before they went out for an evening. Sometimes she feared she would faint.

At 7:05 she plugged in the electric hair-curling wand, turned on the shower, stripped and jumped in. Hurry, hurry. Tom hates to be late. If I'm late he'll be snapping at me all night. Why is everything such a rush? Aren't I good enough? Other women don't seem as hassled as I am. They get everything done without the sweat. Inadequate. Inadequate. It will be different when the kids are older.

Jean was putting in her second pierced earring as Lisann rang the doorbell. Jean smiled slightly as she let the teenager in. Tonight Tom wouldn't be mad. She's ready exactly on time. Jean almost giggled to herself. If anybody can be mad, I can. Tom's still in his underpants. Did she dare make a joke about his being late? Could she laugh and paraphrase what he often said, "Just like a *man*, late again." She'd better not. So few evenings were not wrecked by some kind of fight. This evening still had a chance.

Jean looked up the phone number of the restaurant, left it near the telephone, and gave Lisann some last-minute instructions about Dara's upset stomach. Tom put on his overcoat, leaned down and hugged Kevin, then picked up Dara and held her in his arms. He loved the way the baby felt at night — clean, soft, snuggly, and very adoring. "She's going to be a real flirt," Tom often said. "A real cockteaser. Look at her bat those eyelashes at me." Funny, thought Jean, Kevin used to bat his eyelashes at Tom just like that. Was Kevin going to be a real flirt? Might he turn queer? Jean forced herself to relax. This was a night out and she was going to enjoy it.

How does a Tuesday in the life of Tom and Jean Meyer read to you? Does it seem oppressed? Or does it somewhat approximate your own life?

Sadly, the family life of Tom and Jean is all too common — one of separate worlds. He works at his job. She works at the home and the kids. He supplies the money. She supplies everything else. Based on the chattel system that wife, family, and home are a man's property, Jean serves Tom, does his bidding, and fears that he could throw her out at any time. Tom is not her friend or partner. He is her master. He is master to the children as well.

This situation exists in home after home in America. The mother does the mothering, cooking, cleaning, bottle-washing, and nurturing. The father earns the money — a lonely, pressured, worrisome responsibility — metes out the punishment, and makes decisions about money to be spent and the location of the annual family vacation.

What kind of parenting is done in this kind of home? *All* family members are left wanting. Jean feels abused and put upon that all the child care, housework, management is hers alone. Tom feels harassed that the financial support of four people and a household are his lone responsibility. Each adult feels abandoned, pressured, and angry. The marriage relationship suffers. So do the children.

The children are left with two disgruntled parents, who are unhappy with their lot and with themselves. They are subjected to a mother who is exhausted by the repetitive burdens of house and child care. They are robbed of a relationship with their father. Tom and the Toms all over the country are just not there for their children. A full-time job takes these fathers out of the house five days a week, and financial preoccupation may force them into emotional absence even when they are physically present.

Although Tom genuinely loves the children, he probably never will have an intimate relationship with them. There is no foundation for it. Because Tom never physically cares for the children, he doesn't get to know them. The simple fact that Dara hates carrots, which explains why they end up in her hair rather than in her mouth, is unknown to her father. He has no idea what his kids like, dislike, or are indifferent to. He doesn't know the idiosyncracies that make up their personalities. He doesn't know his kids at all. No wonder he falls back on the sex-role stereotypes of how boys behave and how girls behave when he talks to, and thinks about, Dara and Kevin. Can we excuse Tom because he's merely following the pattern his father showed him?

The absence of men from the physical tasks of caring for

children and running a household have a deleterious effect on the children, on the relationship between parents and children, and on the example children observe of what men and women are capable of. Early on, children extrapolate from their own experience, in their homes and out of them, not only what women do and what men do, but also what women and men can do and are expected to do.

Jean and Tom are patterning Dara and Kevin for their sex-appointed roles for the rest of their lives.

Just down the block from Jean and Tom Meyer live the Spencer-Millers. Their day begins at 6:30 A.M. when baby Blake is up and begging for liberation from the crib. Since it is Robin's morning to get up early so M.J. can sleep a bit, Robin grabs the baby and trundles off to the kitchen for a bottle. At this godforsaken hour it is not unremitting parent-love that keeps Robin awake. It is the sure knowledge that tomorrow morning M.J. will get up with the kids.

Today M.J. will dress five-year-old Jordan for school before dressing for the office. Robin is in charge of the kids during the day and tonight at dinner time. Then M.J. will do the bathing, the story reading, and bedding down.

The schedule at home works quite smoothly now, both parents sharing as equally as possible the maintenance of two small children and the attendant work to run a single-family home. It took some time for the practice to evolve, however.

M.J. and Robin had first made a list of tasks necessary to run the house; then they divided the tasks in half. They made the original list before Jordan was born, when they were both working full time, but the number of jobs had increased with their first child's arrival. Good thing they had worked through their own preconceived notions of what was man's work and what was woman's work before the baby's birth. Otherwise they felt the demands of new parenthood would have thrown them into repeating what their own parents had done. She would have been responsible for the house and the child, he would have been responsible for the money, and they both would have been unhappy. So far, Robin and M.J.

had avoided a sexist breakdown of tasks because they wanted their children to grow up and define themselves by choice rather than letting society define them by sex.

So they divided down the middle such jobs as the laundry, shopping, cleaning, food preparation, mealtime cleanup, contacting babysitters, and making repairs. One week Robin did half and M.J. did the other half. The following week they switched halves.

Years ago they cried and laughed a lot when he couldn't get clothes whiter than white, and she thought a Phillips screwdriver was a brand. There were frustrations, fury, disgust. But with patience, love, and sharing skills with each other, Robin and M.J. learned competence and independence. There are still some jobs she does better than he, some he does better than she. Individual aptitude and skills explain that, however — not what's between their legs.

When Robin and M.J. were a childless couple they considered when and whether to have children of their own. They waited and planned and withstood the pressures of family and friends who urged them to have children — several and soon. They wanted to do things differently from their own parents and knew that would take planning. She didn't want to have to give up her work until the children were in school. He didn't want to miss out on the children's formative years; he wanted a real love relationship with his kids.

The Spencer-Millers considered all of the options. If they both worked full time and hired a housekeeper they felt they wouldn't be parenting. If one worked full time and one stayed home, they'd be back where their parents were, except for a slight variation if she worked and he stayed home. Therefore, they would each have to work part time.

As the author of this perfect life, I will allow my Robin and M.J. to find rewarding and secure three-day-work-week jobs in their chosen fields. The jobs are good and the pay is decent, but because the opportunity for advancement in the years they are working part time is slight, they consider their greatest payment one of time, time with their children when they are small. He has chosen this way of fathering. His own father had worked so many hours a week that he was too exhausted the other hours to enjoy his children, or care for them. Mr. Spencer-Miller has decided to write off money and maybe success, too, to buy a relationship with his children.

Financially their tightest time was the several months after Jordan's birth, when they had only one part-time income. They'd budgeted and saved for those lean months, but there had been a number of unexpected expenditures. Certainly he could have worked full time then, and not started the part-time schedule until she went back to work, but they agreed that was dangerous. Those months could throw them into sexist patterns they might never be able to reverse.

He'd participated in the pregnancy as much as he possibly could. Sometimes Robin and M.J. would howl with laughter at themselves; there are some things men and women just cannot share equally! Through the prepared childbirth classes and from the first labor contraction he'd known about, he acted the participatory parent. Participatory, non-sexist parenthood started with the baby, he felt emphatically — not with the end of the maternity leave. From the beginning, M.J. and Robin shared as equally as possible in the care of their breast-fed baby.

Her mother thought they were odd; his father clearly thought his son was weird. "Do what comes naturally, that's the right thing to do," urged her mother at first. But doing what came naturally, what M.J. and Robin had been conditioned to do, was not what they wanted. So they copied rules and schedules so unnatural and arbitrary at times that the rules often were broken and the schedules abandoned. Nevertheless they maintained a sharing closer to what they considered ideal than if they'd done what came naturally.

Years later their arbitrary, unnatural system had become a way of life that felt quite natural to them, and undeniably natural to their two children. So when the mother is forced out of bed in the morning to feed a hungry baby, there is no muttering, or smoldering resentment that she is always the one to get up. At the Spencer-Miller home there is no master, no slave; no single wage earner and no guilty home worker.

They are partners in parenthood and marriage — equal partners, not one full partner and one junior associate.

With Robin ensconced in a Wednesday-Thursday-Friday job at a newspaper, and M.J. in a Monday-Tuesday-Wednesday job at a school, they each have two days alone with the children. On Wednesday, M.J. works from early morning until mid-afternoon, while Robin has a work shift that ends at 6. For those midday hours they hire a babysitter. But both parents are uneasy about the child care. Will the sitter quit? Call in sick? They feel their success in being sharing, non-sexist parents balances precariously on Wednesday child care. Their system is working out, however, and they consider themselves lucky and deserving because they have planned their lives so carefully.

Let's return to the early morning in the Spencer-Miller home. Robin and Blake are in the kitchen. Jordan and M.J. are in the bathroom, the big one showering, the little one brushing teeth. Jordan usually gets dressed with the working parent in the morning, then after breakfast they go to school together. From school, Robin or M.J. heads off to work.

They most often make the beds before breakfast, but some mornings, when the shoe-tying takes a long time, or a lost button means a last-minute change of outfit, the beds are left for the parent at home to straighten. Today may be one of those days. Jordan wants to thread the new shoelace without help. M.J. is torn between wanting to promote this independence and wanting the shoe tied as quickly as possible. So, there is some coaxing from M.J. for Jordan to make it snappy, or give up the job just this once. Jordan is determined; the independence lesson has been well learned.

With shoes tied, M.J. and Jordan join Blake and Robin for English muffins, eggs, and orange juice. After some discussion of what food M.J. should pick up on the way home from work, M.J. kisses Robin and Blake, grabs Jordan by the hand, and goes out the door.

That evening Robin, Jordan, and Blake are delighted when they hear M.J.'s key turn in the door. After a quick change from business clothes into washable home clothes, M.J.

swoops up the children and carries them off to the bath. Ah, observes M.J., carrots have worked their way into Blake's hair again. Tomorrow I'll try peas.

As Jordan's giggles and Blake's screeches echo in the bathroom, Robin resets the table for the grownups' dinner, tired from a full day with the kids and thankful to deliver them to their other parent. Robin looks forward to spending an evening alone with M.J.

Are you troubled that you don't know what sex the Spencer-Millers are? They aren't confused about what sex they are, even though I've chosen to confuse you. Sex identification is clear for the mother, the father, the daughter, and the son.

The Spencer-Millers have worked out a fairer life than Jean and Tom Meyer's. Soggy towels are not left on the bathroom floor; neither are egg-coated dishes left on the table for the woman to clear. There is a mutual responsibility for the maintenance of life, which the children share. The girl isn't cast in the role of housekeeper-of-tomorrow by her mother. The boy cannot be slovenly because he's male.

How close does your life come to the life the Spencer-Millers lead — a life in which parents are people with interchangeable roles, and tasks and responsibilities are shared? The Spencer-Millers are providing good role models of what women and men can do both in the home and outside.

3

FEMINIST LIFESTYLES

HE Spencer-Millers represent my idea of near perfection in raising non-sexist children. It will be a long time, however, before we have a society of Spencer-Millers.

There are concentrations of feminist families in the big cities, the university towns, and the more obvious settling places of liberal, progressive parents. But the small towns usually have only one or two "town feminists" who can in any way affect childraising or child-educating policies. Most people in this country are mired in sex-role stereotypes, not realizing that removing the limits that stereotypes impose on human potential would not shatter the world as they know it. Until legislation promoting equal rights for both sexes is passed and multiple court cases are won, a non-sexist education and upbringing will continue to be a gift only from fair-minded parents and educators, not the right of every child.

Our culture is having a hard time dealing with adult liberation, be it freedom of the races or freedom of the sexes. Our culture is even more resistant to a liberation for children. We have quite rigid stereotypes of what little girls and little boys are made of and how they differ from one another.

In the summer of 1976 there was a brouhaha over a Department of Health, Education, and Welfare ruling that banned Father-and-Son banquets and Mother-and-Daughter teas in Scottsdale, Arizona. No lesser official than the President of the United States, Gerald Ford, acted in favor of these sex-exclusive affairs, as though he felt there is something sacred about the way we've been ushering our children into life.

Children's liberation is proceeding very slowly. Psychiatrist Robert E. Gould, head of the Mental Health Center at Metropolitan Hospital in New York City, thinks that an ideal world "is not going to happen for the generation that are children today." There is hope, however, for as Gould points out, "if we have to go 90 percent from where we are, if they go 20 or 25, it will be that much easier for the next generation."

For those of us trying to raise non-sexist children in the here and now, the long view that a non-sexist society simply will evolve is of little solace.

Children usually repeat the living patterns they learn from their parents. In order for a non-sexist society to come about, these patterns must be broken. Realizing this, feminist families are experimenting with a variety of lifestyles in an attempt to find one that is both workable for them and an effective model for their children. These attempts range from disposing of the nuclear family entirely to making minor adjustments in the division of responsibilities for child care and household chores.

Some feminist parents, unhappy with the isolated nuclear family upbringing they experienced, have chosen to bring their children up within a group. They have created non-related extended families that combat sex stereotyping and provide a participatory community for their children. As part of life in any family there are jobs to be done regularly. Food preparation, dishes, cleaning, laundry, and shopping are a few. If only two grownups share the load there is plenty for each daily. But in a group, with chores split six, eight, or even ten ways, there is less work for mother and for father. Everybody works.

Some group living situations have established a rotating schedule of people and chores, where every grownup must do every job. For example, in House A, George may love cooking but loathe laundry. Like it or not, George must take his turn at the washing machine. Other living situations are less rigid. For example, if George lived in House B, he could trade away his laundry chores to Sally, who'd rather deal with ground-in dirt than ground meat any day. But even loathsome, tedious chores are less offensive once in fourteen days than fourteen times in fourteen days.

Group living also offers children the chance to learn that household chores are not sex-linked. "The kids see men prepare meals routinely. They see guys fold laundry and use the vacuum cleaner. Pitching in is part of living here. It is part of just plain living," said a parent. "Politically, I think it is important that the men learn how to run the house. Sometimes it has been hard to stick with my politics. We've had some terrible meals," admitted a woman.

"I have to admit I love to see the guys doing the shit work. My own father sat on his ass while my mother cleaned around him. I'm tempted to scold the guys for not getting my clothes 'whiter than white,' but my laundry may come out grey next week," said another woman.

"The children watch the men prepare meals for the whole group. In even moderately liberated households men don't do the cooking for a dinner party, or a big group. A father may cook meals for the kids, or even for the whole family once in a while, but the mother cooks for company. It is not that way here. My daughter will not grow up thinking cooking is a female job," commented a mother.

"I'm living here because it is easier for me as a single parent with a boy child. He is my responsibility, but sometimes I can exhange child care hours for other services with somebody here in the house. When I am sick I know there is someone to care for Josh. When we lived alone I had the flu. In the morning I put Josh on my bed with me, got some crackers and juice, turned on the tube, and prayed we'd get through the day. It was horrible.

"Also, there are men in this house and that is important for Josh. They are men who are developing relationships with him, independent of their relationship with me. He needs a father figure, or two. There is no man in my life. There should be some in his."

The children within these group communities have a unique opportunity to interact with other children in an intimate atmosphere without the conflicts of sibling rivalry.

"Our son is really very sweet and nurturing with the baby upstairs. He pats the baby, tells us when the baby cries, and is very interested in the kid's development. Josh knows the baby goes upstairs at night. He doesn't have to share his parents with him."

"One of the reasons we live in a group is money. It is cheaper to live here, splitting the costs, than to live alone. I don't think I could make enough money working part time that could support our life, and leave me enough time for the kids. The money pressure is off," said a father.

Some feminist parents, whether they live in a group or in a single family unit, are also reaching out to day-care centers to provide alternative lifestyles for their children. But many of them are also finding that the resources for quality day care are often not available. Day care is not a high priority item in the United States, though the need is there and growing every day.

Twelve to fifteen years ago, there were fewer than 200,000 licensed day-care center spaces available nationwide. In 1972 (the last year with reliable national data), however, there were 1,021,202 day-care spaces. Since 1972 the number has grown as parents establish their own cooperative centers to fill their needs.

"I think we have a terrific advantage in raising a non-sexist child. We were involved in running the day-care center where she spent eight hours, five days a week of her life. Her peers at two and three began to balance what she got at home. The day-care center was tremendously creative in dealing with sexism. What you say. How you deal with each other. Who does what. Who brings whom to school. The men did the cooking at the center, too. We had real impact on her life as non-sexist parents," reports a mother.

Parents who are committed to day care are quick to point out the advantages of good group care for young children: when day care is available, parents and children are not locked in a one-to-one grip of tension and boredom and dependence; kids are exposed to good models of both sexes, the parents say, and have a good chance of escaping sex-role stereotyping; the children have a good group experience early in a warm environment that is like a second home. "Being in good day care beats being at home with the television, the toys, and Mommy," said one young advocate.

Many day-care parents also extol the constancy of a center. "I don't have to worry if the sitter is going to show up, or not. I take Jen to the center. If someone is sick there, they hire a substitute. I can make appointments and know I can keep them," said a mother.

Parents with good day-care experiences are quick to proselytize. They say how happy and well adjusted their children are. They speak of joyous reunion after hours of separation. "She's in her own world with her own friends at the day care. The environment is stimulating. At home she'd be bored," claimed a mother.

"Someday we'll all have day-care centers in our neighborhoods. They'll be like churches, or meeting halls, or, yes, student centers. They will be resources for parents and children in the community, supported by tax dollars. When? Someday," projected another parent.

Feminist parents with children in day care don't feel guilty about leaving their children for hours during the day. They sincerely believe they are fulfilling the responsibilities of parenting and, in addition, changing the social order of mother-child fusion.

The culture, however, does not support these parents. They are a minority. They are a counterculture in a society that believes that mother and child are inextricably bound until nursery school or kindergarten separates them for three hours a day! A primary parent who does not have to work to put food on the table may therefore experience ambivalence and indecision about day care, nursery school, home care, and other choices that are available.

One day-care teacher said, "We try to offer nurturant care for young children and some guilt-free time for their parents. There aren't many places a woman with, say, about $15,000 a year coming in can take her child for day care. She's been told by the media and everybody else to stay home. We tell her it is all right to go out."

Our society is not set up for day care. If parents are unable to find a cooperative, they often are forced to pay dearly for quality daytime care. One feminist couple who between them hold a job and a half say they spend $4,000 a year on child care for their four-year-old and eighteen-month-old. The older child is in private school, the younger in a private day-care center a couple days a week, and one day a week they pay a long-day babysitter. Their priority is good care and quality schooling for their children. It costs.

Those who are unable to find quality day care and instead choose home care for young children are concerned about the reality that 97.8 percent of the private household workers in this country are women. The numbers show children that housework and child work are women's work.

Professional male housekeepers exist, but seldom outside of television and the movies. Sebastian Cabot played a nur-turant housekeeper for a single parent and children for years. Fred MacMurray had the good luck to find an Oriental male housekeeper to help him care for his three sons and his pro-gram's ratings. A movie series featuring a Mr. Belvedere — a kind of male Mary Poppins — showed us the acerbic sweet-ness of a British nanny. We've laughed with and loved these characters. But when real-life families hire housekeepers for their children they hire women. Male housekeepers are crea-tions of Hollywood; they are not to be found through em-ployment agencies. Couples who hire female housekeepers thus provide their children with another example that wom-an's place is in the home.

One woman who worked between the births of her two children and began a second career several months after her second was born admitted she worried somewhat about her son's image of women. The female housekeeper "serves him, does for him, provides for both kids. But they know that Pat gets paid for her work, that she has hours of work and hours when she leaves, goes home, and has time off. Jake knows Pat is not always on call. It is different from the traditional idea of women in the home. When my son grows up he will realize that from a time shortly after he was born his mother was out of the house working."

"I worked part time till my youngest was three," explained another working mother. "I was offered this job as a full-time counselor in this terrific, premier school system. I hired a Mary Poppins, a twenty-two-year-old wonder who papered walls, did laundry, bought Christmas presents, shopped, cooked, played, who was with us for three years. She came in at 7:30 in the morning and stayed until five.

"I was spared the nightmare of day care — there is some good and some terrible. I had enough money to bypass that. Our housekeeper was in many ways a surrogate mother. I was hiring a replacement for me.

"My kids have classism. Women have the right to work, they believe. But they know that educated women have more options. Now we have a young woman in graduate school who lives on the top floor in our house. She does child care and feeds our plants in exchange for the room.

"All that nice egalitarianism takes a certain amount of money."

Even though these parents admit they are reinforcing the stereotype of woman-as-home-worker by hiring a female housekeeper, they fight the stereotype after working hours. "If Jane were to come home and take over all the chores after our housekeeper left, the kids would certainly decide that housework is woman's work. But I'm right in there when I get home. We share what there is to do to get the kids fed, cleaned up, and into bed. When Jane is out for the night, I take over. When I'm out, she does the caretaking," said one father.

Families without access to a good day-care center, or without the need or resources to hire a full-time housekeeper, must bear the burden of finding reliable part-time child care. "It is a nightmare to find the perfect part-time person. We must have gone through five sitters last year. That's terrible for a child, and awful for us. It makes me feel very insecure about working. I can't afford to hire somebody full time, but not that many women want to work only a few days a week taking care of my child. They need more money to live," said one mother speaking for many.

"The other morning my sitter didn't show up. I was to start a new job that morning. I called her house. I even sent a telegram. Nothing. She just vanished. I had checked her references, and she was terrific with the baby, then poof. Gone. Now my husband and I have decided to alternate staying home if the sitter doesn't show. I wonder how it will work out. He has a full-time job," worried a mother. Another mother added, "Sometimes I think working is not worth the aggravation. It might be easier to give up and retire to my kitchen and bake bread."

Like housekeepers, most babysitters are female. But more males are babysitting than ever before, for a variety of reasons. Some say that young girls are not sitting because the women's movement has made them scorn house- and child work. Some think boys are babysitting because they cannot find other work. Others think single mothers want to bring a male figure into the home. Another reason some parents seek out male babysitters is safety, feeling that a sturdy male would be better able to ward off an intruder than an attractive female would be.

There is a definite increase in the demand for boy sitters, according to Elizabeth O'Malley, executive director of the Nutley (New Jersey) Family Service Bureau. She thinks the increase in one-parent families is one reason why boy sitters are requested to care for young children. Another reason may be that parents feel the use of male babysitters helps fight sex-role stereotyping.

But even after parents have decided on their babysitter's or housekeeper's sex, they must often make their peace with their employee's politics. "I always sound out a sitter about sexism. If somebody is rigid about what boys and girls can't do because of their sex, I don't hire them. That is, if I can get someone else," said a mother.

A number of parents said they routinely instruct their sitters about sexism, try to raise the sitters' consciousnesses, and sometimes put the sitters to the test. "If a sitter tells a little boy not to cry, I won't hire her. Not because she's sexist, but because she's probably a cold person," said a parent. "I don't think about sexism and sitters too much anymore. I am so thankful to get a responsive energetic person, I figure the kids can survive whatever sexist assaults come their way," said another parent.

"At first we instructed the sitter what to do and say and what not to do and say. We shared how we felt about women and sexism. But what was happening was all the spontaneity was going out of the relationship between that woman and our child," said a father. "Warmth and affection are more important than politics."

In fact, one psychiatrist warned against such rigid interaction between caretaker and child: "If you are very militant about anything, you may do a bad job in proselytizing and get more raw emotion and anger involved than rational good sense or tolerance. The whole manner in which you treat the child, or feel for the child, is most important. You can do the right thing but with the wrong spirit, and get nowhere and hurt the child. The relationship with the child is what's really important."

Couples who have chosen to practice non-sexist childraising and live their lives differently from the way their parents lived say they sometimes feel like the odd-couple-out.

"When we first started this switch — me working full time and Mark working part time — we were very excited about it and eager to share," said one mother. "However, couples we talked with thought we were criticizing them, when we were just sharing. At work, very few of my colleagues understand that Mark works part time so that he can be with the kids. They can't conceive of a lifestyle that could be that way. They are uncomfortable when I talk about our situation. They tend to back off. There are not that many people I am comfortable with. I've become more cautious, quieter about sharing because of the initial reaction we had."

"But," says Mark, "we are learning and our children are learning that you can appreciate other people, even if they are very different from you. When you are dealing with friends you can't be hypercritical. You can't expect friends to be exactly like you. If you criticize them, or try to make them like you, you end the relationship. We find we are changing the people around us. Friends correct their own sexist language around us. Just the other day, somebody said, 'See that kid run like a boy, um, er, like a child.' "

Not only our peers, but grandparents, too, often question the theory and practice of non-sexist childraising. Grandparents sometimes fear that upsetting the order of the sex roles and changing the culture will ruin their grandchildren. At the same time they wonder why the way they raised their families is under attack.

"Families are very influential," said one psychiatrist in one of the biggest understatements ever made. "They exert terrific pressure. You just have to learn how to deal with it."

Some feminist parents have explained to their own parents why they are raising their children differently, but most have considered the issue too highly charged to deal with.

"My mother — now that is the area I haven't taken up," said a mother speaking for others. "I've thought of things I want her to read, because as much as I say I still don't think it carries any weight. She buys him trucks and balls and says things like, 'What a little boy!' With Lynn she buys long dresses. At first I would challenge every move, but I wouldn't carry through. I wouldn't sit down and show her what the implications are."

"I can't talk about it with my mother because I don't want to talk with her, I want to scream at her," admitted a mother. "So I don't explain what we are doing. I just do it. When Jenny was still in the carriage my mother and I were wheeling her on the street. I leaned over and kissed Jenny and told her what a terrific person she was. My mother asked me, 'Don't you ever tell her she's a girl?' As if Jenny will miss the point. I wanted to punch her."

"My parents decided we were odd when we wanted to live in the city, even after the children were born. So anything we do is considered odd."

"My father says that Joy is becoming more like a boy every day. He's just observing, not judging. We don't talk theory with him."

Even the grandparents, or potential grandparents, who understand non-sexist childraising are ambivalent about it. One educator said, "I want my daughter to have a career, but I don't want her to go off and leave my grandchild, either."

Of course, some couples who believe in non-sexist childraising are unable to live other than a traditional life because of sheer economics. If the mother has no marketable skills and the father does, and there are three children to support, it is quite certain that he will be working full time and she will be at home, filling the traditional role of child tender and homemaker. But must they give up hopes of raising non-sexist children? Feminist politics or not, they are living the stereotype. How can this kind of couple combat sexism since they are not modeling a non-sexist life?

Psychiatrist Robert E. Gould suggests, "The next best thing is to teach non-sexism, even if you are not living it. The woman should explain to the kids, 'Look, for the past forty years I've been living this way. I was taught this way. I didn't train myself for a profession. The only thing I can really do well is housework and bringing up children. If I had my life to live over again, I would opt for a different course. My husband was brought up his way. If he had to do it again, he would do this and this. . . . But we can't really change all that much, but we feel there is a better way for you.'

"Parents who smoke and say, 'I really shouldn't smoke. Smoking is bad, but I really can't stop' — now that's not as good as the parent who is able to give up smoking, but it is still better than the parent who still smokes and tries to justify it, or hide from the kid that this is a weakness on their part. The parent who can't do the right thing, but admits it, can expose the youngster to other ways of living than the stereotype."

Gould also suggests that parents seek out examples of alternative lifestyles. "If you can't live the right way, expose your child to training and other models who will give the kid examples of how to live differently," he urges. Find friends and acquaintances who live another way. Somewhere in your sphere there is a mother who works full time and one or two who work part time. There are also men who are full-time homemakers, though they are a rarer breed. Look for men who work part time so they can spend more time with the children. If living examples of alternative lifestyles aren't available to you and your children, look in the press. The magazines and newspapers run features about people who are switching roles, forging a new way to live.

Pick a school where the sexes are treated fairly. If you are not in the private-school market, pressure your public school for shop courses and home-economics courses for both sexes. Pressure for coed sports. Organize a sex-roles study group of parents and teachers.

Look for women and men in non-stereotyped jobs. Bring women painters, plumbers, and carpenters into your home to work. Hire male housecleaners and male babysitters. Seek out women doctors and dentists. "We have one doctor of each sex. A female pediatrician for the baby, and a male for our older child. When my own dentist retires, I'm going to a female dentist. I thought it would be hard to find, but all I did was open the phone book. There is a whole bunch of them," said a father. "Sometimes I make a big deal out of the fact that a woman is doing a job that a man usually does, sometimes I don't. I don't want Sara to think it is odd that a woman is, say, a doctor. I want her to think it is regular and possible for her," said a mother.

The father in a family that is living the stereotyped life has a special responsibility to involve himself in total care of the children, if he is truly committed to raising non-sexist children. "Even if a man works nine to five, it doesn't mean he can't pitch in wholeheartedly when he is home," offered one feminist. Assuming total care is the key to showing children that men can be caretakers, too. If papa has to wake mama up to ask her what baby eats for breakfast, that baby will get the idea that mama is mama to them all. If the father can't dress the child unless the mother has laid out the clothes, that child will learn that the father is just a helper.

With both parents paying continuous attention to the examples they are setting for their children, progress can be made toward a society such as the Spencer-Millers represent.

4

PARTICIPATORY CHILDBIRTH

GUIDING a child away from sexism begins before a child is born. Today couples who want to raise non-sexist human beings are turning to methods of childbirth that allow women and men to share the beginning of parenthood as fully as possible. Feminist fathers-to-be are trying to involve themselves in their wives' pregnancies. These same men are struggling against a strong tradition of no involvement.

Consider the stereotype in the American way of pregnancy and birth. The drama begins with a pastel-dressed wife who first makes her husband comfortable in his easy chair before she announces, "We're going to have a wee one." Despite his reclining position, the husband faints. He is shocked by the news.

When he regains consciousness and a degree of composure, he leaps up and offers her his chair. "You'd better take it easy from now on, sweetie." There is a lot of blushing from both parties.

The wife remains serene and controlled for the duration of the pregnancy. The husband takes on the role of bumbling messenger boy, running hither and thither in the middle of the night in pursuit of pickles and ice cream to satisfy the archetypal pregnant woman's cravings.

Suddenly, one night, she awakens him with an "Oops, I think this is it." Despite his supine position, the husband faints. With recovery he becomes frantic, races into the car and leaves his wife to follow, carrying her own suitcase. He runs the traffic lights on the way to the hospital, ignorant of

31

the duration of labor and fearing delivery in the car. His now-laboring wife is worried about him, for the stereotypic American husband-in-labor is a nervous wreck.

At the hospital the wife is spirited away, urging her husband not to worry — she'll see him when IT is over. He is left to pace in the hospital waiting room for hours, separated from his genuinely loved wife and his imminent child, until the obstetrician arrives to announce, "It's a girl" or "It's a boy." The husband faints again.

This is the typical role the American husband plays during his wife's pregnancy and the birth of his child: except for presence at conception, there is no role. The message that comes across from television, movies, and books is loud and clear — men, keep out.

Until the advent of prepared childbirth in this country fifteen years ago, fathers didn't even touch their children until mother and child were released from the hospital. For the duration of the hospital stay, which sometimes stretched to ten days, fathers waved to their newborns through nursery windows. No touching. No kissing. And sadly, no bonding and finding a way into each other's lives.

Even if a new mother was ignorant about child care, she had the length of her hospital stay to learn some of the basics under the nurses' guidance. She practiced mothering skills and in the time allowed to her by the often rigid hospital schedules, she got to know her child. During visiting hours she would tell her husband about his child. All his information about the child, his child, was secondhand, funneled either through his wife or the hospital staff. He gobbled up whatever news they shared, but he couldn't help feeling left out. There was no place for him in the baby's life.

During the hospital stay a bad pattern evolved that most families never broke. Just as the pregnancy and birth had been the woman's experience alone, the newborn child became hers alone also. The hospital only reinforced what the society believed — that children are women's work, women's exclusive preserve, and there is no place for fathers.

Feminist families overwhelmingly have rejected the "cut the

couple apart, knock the woman out, then pull the kid out" school of childbearing. Instead they have sought out, pressured for, and embraced the childbirth methods that allow families to be conscious and together. Prepared childbirth methods allow a valuable place for the expectant father and provide an active, dignified role for the mother. Parenthood begins with birth, these couples believe.

By far the most popular method of prepared childbirth used in this country is the psychoprophylactic or Lamaze technique. With origins in the Soviet Union and France, the Lamaze method uses Pavlovian psychological methods to reteach brains and bodies how to respond to pain. Instead of tensing in fear at the onset of a labor contraction, a woman is conditioned to respond instead with a rehearsed breathing pattern and relaxation.

Thank You, Dr. Lamaze, by Marjorie Karmel, was published in this country in 1959. The book is an account of the author's own American-in-Paris psychoprophylactic delivery by Dr. Fernand Lamaze. The next year, Mrs. Elisabeth Bing and a number of obstetricians formed the American Society for Psychoprophylaxis in Obstetrics (ASPO).

Over the next ten years ASPO increased its membership slowly but steadily. In 1971, however, it grew dramatically, doubling its membership. By 1974 membership was up another 32 percent, and by 1976 the 1974 membership had doubled, burgeoning to 3,350 in number. In 1975, 87,500 students took the Lamaze childbirth courses.

Why the dramatic growth in the early seventies after only moderate increases for a decade? ASPO spokeswoman Melba Gandy put it this way: "I think the women's movement is largely responsible for the tremendous growth. Women no longer want some damn doctor to pat them on the head and say, 'Dear, dear, I'll wake you when it's over.' Women want an active part in what's happening to their lives and their bodies. Families have come to regard childbirth as an experience, one of the great ones, a super one for the joy of the family."

"We hear over and over again the notion from men that 'I want to share equally in the birth experience' — as equally, of course as they possibly can," reports Joanna Shulman, a New Jersey Lamaze instructor turned medical student.

During the last fifteen years, while ASPO membership has grown by leaps and bounds, the only male members of ASPO have been the obstetricians and health-care professionals. The teaching of the Lamaze method of childbirth has been left almost exclusively to women. Of 2,500 teachers trained in the last fourteen-and-one-half years only three have been men. In the last six months, however, ten men have applied for teacher training. Of the ten, two are practicing physicians.

According to Melba Gandy, one doctor wants to be a Lamaze teacher because he feels there are "no acceptable prepared childbirth classes" in his area. The other doctor feels his current role in the life of the expectant couple is too limited. He thinks the doctor-patient relationship will open up if he is in a teaching relationship with his couples. He anticipates that his being a teacher will open the couples up to him and let him share their hopes, their fears, their dreams in a way they are hiding from him now. The eight other male ASPO teaching applicants are fathers who participated in their own children's Lamaze deliveries. All but one of the eight plans to team teach with a woman. Some will teach with their wives.

One of those couples is Susan and Gary Kwiatkowski of Jersey City, New Jersey. She's a former Peace Corps worker and high school science teacher. He's an ex-Peace Corpsman as well, and currently an undertaker. When the Kwiatkowskis expressed an interest in sharing the value of Lamaze, Elisabeth Bing suggested they team teach. After all, men and women together are responsible for the event of childbirth, even though until recently fathers generally have been excluded.

Among the other Lamaze teacher applicants is a political scientist who is working in social research. He wants to discover when children form opinions about birth. He wants to figure out a way of getting to children early, so they form good opinions. Another man is a sociologist. Another is a psychologist at a university.

By and large, these male Lamaze applicants did not anticipate sexism, an ASPO spokeswoman commented. The only
remark about possible sex-prejudice came from the one male
applicant who plans to teach childbirth classes alone. He felt
the intake interviewers who examine every potential teacher
were "particularly rough on me."

Perhaps prepared childbirth, with the husband in atten-
dance, is our culture's way of providing a ritual that includes
men in childbirth. The custom of the couvade is found in different parts of our world. From the French verb *couver*, meaning "to brood or hatch," couvade is a ceremony, a "laboring"
the father acts out. He experiences, or acts as if he is ex-
periencing, labor contractions and is attended by men of his
community while the women care for the laboring wife. Until
the last fifteen years the men in this country labored alone,
pacing a hospital waiting room, while the women labored
alone, under medication, often strapped into their beds. Now
more parents-to-be work *together* to deliver their child.

Childbirth is a major event in which many men want to participate. Psychological case studies detail little boys' imaginary
pregnancies. In mythology, Zeus's frustration and jealousy of
his wife's uterus drove him to swallow her so he could bear
her child. George Gilder, in his 1973 book *Sexual Suicide*, a de-
fense of male chauvinism, also details uterine envy.

Feminist husbands don't relegate childbearing to the realm
of the wife. Some of them are very up front about feeling left
out, frustrated, and jealous. One father I interviewed spoke
of his frustration in not knowing how it felt to be pregnant.
"I read all the books, talked to our female friends, even asked
my mother. I have some idea now, but I'll *never know* what it's
like to be pregnant." Other fathers admitted envy for their
wives' "magical," "mystical" experience.

Is it jealousy of female physical creativity that motivates
male obstetricians to rob women of an active role in delivery?
With the introduction of "twilight sleep" in 1902, when
obstetricians administered morphine and scopolamine in
combination, women could be delivered of children without
any conscious memory of the event. They were promised a

painless, memory-less childbirth by their physicians. Almost all of the women assented. How ironic that the female suffragists early in this century so willingly embraced chloroform and later twilight sleep to liberate them from what they considered the biological oppression of childbirth. The feminists today have battled for control of their own bodies, control of their own childbirth.

Twilight sleep robbed women of an active role in birth, and left them passive, to be delivered by a masterful wielder of scalpel and forceps. With the help of medicine, the woman and her doctor, who was most often a man, were recast in the traditional roles of he-active, she-passive.

When women wanted to reclaim their active role in childbirth, and include the fathers of their children, they met with much resistance from the Old Guard of the obstetrical field, who seemed to say, "Birthing babies is a medical affair, not a family affair." Physicians were reluctant to relinquish their all-powerful role and leave the spotlight to the laboring mother-to-be and attendant father-to-be.

Arguments against the fathers' presence in the delivery rooms were manifold. With no consideration for his rights as a father, his desire to bond with his child at birth, or begin parenthood as a participant, a father was treated as unnecessary. He was told that it was downright unnatural for a man to be involved in what was woman's work — he'd be trouble, maybe faint, perhaps contaminate the sterile area, spread germs, get in the way, or wreak some kind of havoc.

Some "authorities" even assert that a husband's presence at delivery could spell disaster for the couple's marriage and sex life. Dr. Waldo Fielding, a leading medical opponent of prepared childbirth, warns in his 1962 book, *The Childbirth Challenge,* that even if a delivery is routine "an untrained observer, particularly an anxious husband, can never be adequately prepared for the frighteningly unfamiliar sounds and sights of even the normal process of childbirth." The prepared-childbirth father is not the "untrained observer" that Fielding labels him, however.

Seattle physician, Dr. Robert H. Stewart, is also opposed to husbands' participating in childbirth. In the November 1963 issue of *Medical Times,* he wrote, "The male attitude to the female genitalia is one of unconscious hostility. To him the charm of a woman is her mystery. It is inconceivable that a normal male watching the delivery of his wife could experience anything but revulsion at the vision of these genitalia under the worst and filthiest conditions." He claims that prepared childbirth has caused a "breakdown of hospital techniques . . . and produced an orgy of sadism and masochism into the sacred privilege of motherhood." Women who were drugged, abandoned in a semi-waking–semi-sleeping state, then forcibly delivered of their children might well argue with Stewart's definition of "orgy of sadism and masochism."

Although the arguments against fathers' participating in births have been disproven repeatedly, there are still holdouts. In 1972, I was given the following reasons why my husband would not be allowed in the delivery room at University Hospital in New York City. The obstetrician, a woman of about fifty, explained that I would be the most important person in that delivery room. She couldn't risk my safety to have him present. He might distract her, or faint, or contaminate the room. Then she added her own reason why I should be separated from the father of my child. "Anyway," she said, "you won't look so good then. He shouldn't see you." In other words, I should preserve at all costs my place as a decorative object. Protect him by pretending that birth is medical magic, not hard work. And rob him of taking part in the beginning of his fatherhood. We changed doctors and hospitals.

Shortly thereafter University Hospital changed its policy, and today every major hospital in the borough of Manhattan tolerates or encourages participation. "However," reports Lamaze instructor Joanna Shulman, "the minute you step outside that borough you start running into trouble."

In the last three or four years many more hospitals have come around. The birthrate is down, and hospitals are competing for maternity patients. They must offer what the customer wants.

Prepared, participatory childbirth is not yet commonplace

in the United States, however. According to an ASPO spokeswoman, "The major centers are clustered along both coasts and in the big cities in the middle. Everybody is not doing it."

But more and more couples every year *are* doing it. The September 1976 issue of *Mothers' Manual* polled its readership, and reported that 74 percent of its readers chose prepared childbirth. Of that percentage, 81 percent picked the Lamaze method. And of that percentage, 87 percent of the fathers were in the delivery room.

How different a picture from only five years ago. In the last few years men have become as vehement as women about the importance of participatory childbirth and parenthood. Because they were active at the birth of their children, these fathers feel much closer and more involved in their children's lives than do the absent, though still concerned, parents of less than a generation ago.

Not only does participatory childbirth alter the child-parent relationship, but it undeniably betters the relationship between wife and husband. Since prepared childbirth requires a coordination, a team effort, couples speak of increased mutual respect for each other.

"I never knew women were so strong," a very new father told me. "She was like a superwoman. At one point I wanted to give up — the labor was moving so slowly. But she hung in there." And a man who has had two children by prepared childbirth marveled, "I never thought women were weaklings, but I know I thought they were weaker. Now I know the strength in man and woman is just distributed differently. Show me a man with a muscle like the uterus!"

Despite the resurgence of feminism and the growth of trust between the sexes that some couples experience, prejudices remain. "Well into labor," one East Coast woman told me, "I was still afraid John would let me down, fall apart and leave me all alone. I'd been fed all that nonsense that men are really weak and untrustworthy, that they can't take it. Before labor I trusted him, but in the crunch, I was afraid he'd turn and run. And I knew I'd hate him forever if he did.

"We were both nervous. But John was there for me. He never thought of leaving. I could never have done it all without him. Now I trust him implicitly. I trust him with my life. Before, I didn't realize childbirth was a way of testing John. It turned out that way. John passed with flying colors."

A Boston woman told me her already sharing marital relationship was much improved since their daughter was born. "I've loved my husband more. He was there for me during a terribly long labor, then we were a family in the delivery room."

Many feminist couples spoke of the immediate sense of family they felt in the delivery room: "After they sewed me up they left the three of us together alone in the delivery room. We just held her, and looked at her, and cried. Here was our baby, and we were a family." This same mother says that this feeling has carried over since the birth of their child five years ago.

One father shared his altered view of his infant daughter, other baby girls, his wife, and all other women. Like so many others, this man talked about strength: "My eight-pound daughter will grow up and be able to deliver children. That requires enormous strength. Endurance. I'm going to remember Barbara's power in delivery every time someone tells me girls are weak."

However, no amount of propaganda from couples who've been through childbirth together can convince a pregnant woman that gestation and childbirth are a completely shared experience. In some ways the experience is intensely isolated and introspective. What woman who has physically surrendered herself to pregnancy and the inescapable event of childbirth hasn't felt some terror that she, in the end, will be alone with the unknown? Steeped with folklore that childbirth is woman's curse since Eve bit the apple, and coupled with one horror story after another from sisters and mothers and cousins and aunts, pregnant women hope sincerely that there is a better way.

The combination of prepared childbirth, a supportive physician or midwife, and a first-quality delivery facility or hospital take much of the loneliness and fear out of delivering a baby. It places delivery in the realm of participation, a joint effort by family and professionals that bonds a nuclear family together from the beginning. It takes the father out of the waiting room and places him in the action, where today's feminist father wants to be.

Among feminist families in the last ten years the home delivery has gained popularity and in some places an almost chic with-it-ness. In some parts of the country where participatory childbirth is still scorned by physicians and hospitals, couples have chosen home delivery out of desperation. It is the only way they can assume any control over what they feel should be undeniably a family experience. Certain realities, however, dampen my enthusiasm for home delivery. What if an infant can't breathe and needs to be resuscitated? What if the umbilical cord is caught around the infant's neck? What if the placenta separates prematurely?

Despite these risks, home delivery is a choice some couples are making. The story of Betty and Frank is a case in point. Frank had refused induction into the armed forces in opposition to the United States involvement in the Vietnamese War and had spent twenty-seven months in a federal prison. Betty and Frank before, during, and after his imprisonment were not keen on institutions, including hospitals. They wanted a home delivery. They wanted non-sexist childraising. They found an osteopath who would do a home delivery. He had a back-up hospital there in St. Louis, about five minutes away from their house.

Surprisingly Betty went into labor seven weeks before her due date. The home delivery of tiny Rachel was fine. The family bonded together, just as they hoped, but she was very tiny, very young, very premature, and they were worried about her survival.

The doctor was more worried about Rachel's unborn sibling. Undetected, Betty was pregnant with twins. So with a minutes-old child in their arms, Betty and Frank and their physician barreled across town to the back-up hospital. Jessica was born a half-hour later. When they arrived at the hospital,

Frank was told he couldn't enter the sterile area. The doctor intervened, told Frank to scrub up, and reunited the family unit. Meanwhile, Betty had been stripped of her nightgown and lay naked on a table as they doused her "with some brown, cold horrible liquid." "I was all stained. They looked at me as if I were some terrible dirty person," remembers Betty.

"There was no comparison between the two births," she says. "At the hospital they really freaked me out. I'd do a home birth again, if there is a next time. I don't think I'd have a doctor there. He really didn't help us at the birth." The babies spent their first month in the hospital until they were strong enough to come home.

For those of us who are frightened of home delivery, but reject hospital delivery, there is a compromise. San Francisco General Hospital offers an alternative birth center that will discharge mothers and new babies from twelve to twenty-four hours after birth. Babies are delivered in cozy, home-like rooms, complete with rocking chairs. Mothers can deliver in their beds and keep their babies with them. Children of the expectant couple can be present at the birth, as well as the couple's own siblings and parents. In the event of any complications the attending midwife can call on the rest of the professional staff and all the modern technology a hospital offers.

The popularity of alternative birth centers is growing. There is a childbirth center operating in Manhattan. Even standard hospitals are bending about enforced hospitalization of a mother and baby after an uncomplicated birth. Georgetown University Hospital in Washington, D.C., and Mount Sinai Hospital in New York are among the facilities that discharge mother and baby quickly, sometimes as soon as six hours after birth.

The positive aspects of this kind of delivery are money, time, and safety. Costs are down for a family since there is no lengthy hospital stay. The home life is not interrupted for a long period of time. A family with another small child at home can be reunited quickly. And finally, delivery is within the safe boundaries of a hospital.

5

FEMALE CHAUVINISM

 TREMENDOUS sense of pride has developed among women, and like-thinking men, for that which is female. The power of positive thinking and genuine pride has aided blacks, Native Americans, and women. Ova power is to be respected.

Children with ova power are, in certain circles, even preferred. Women are saying that females are valuable, after ages of worthlessness. Historically female infanticide was commonplace. Hebrew scholar Raphael Patai, cited in Adrienne Rich's *Of Woman Born*, quotes from the Koran a father who asks about his newborn daughter: "Shall he keep it in contempt, or bury it in the dust?" Patai reports that "we know from historical documents relating to the Arab world from prehistoric times down to the nineteenth century that often a father decided to put to death a daughter either immediately upon her birth or at a later date. The usual method of putting a newborn daughter to death was to bury her in the sands of the desert." Scholar Lloyd deMause, in his *History of Childhood*, theorizes that the imbalance of men over women from ancient times to the Middle Ages was caused by the practice of killing baby girls. "Even a rich man always exposes a daughter." A first-century man writing to his wife said, "If as well may happen, you give birth to a child, if it is a boy let it live; if it is a girl, expose it."

With this kind of history, no wonder women long preferred male children. Who would want to gestate a fetus for nine months, feel its flippings grow to rumblings under the stretched skin, labor and deliver, only to have the child, if it be a girl, be treated like a reject? After all that work, women wanted to produce a valued product, not a child to be summarily killed.

For ages and ages men have hoped for rebirth in the persons of sons. Women seldom were encouraged in that dream. Now the dreams of women are being realized. There is celebration upon the birth of a daughter.

For those of us who were pregnant in the early 1970s, giving birth to a daughter was the feminist dream. In the Decade of the Woman, our daughters would be our heiresses.

Throughout my pregnancy for my daughter, Casey, I wanted a girl. Certainly I wanted a healthy, complete, happy baby. But that wasn't all. I wanted that perfect creature to be a girl. What a reverse of the stereotype my husband and I were. Instead of hoping for a son, someone to carry on the name, someone to play ball with, someone to teach what it is like to be a man, fruit of his loins with a penis, Jeff just wanted a healthy baby. Either sex would do. Either sex would delight. My vocal preference for a daughter was female chauvinism to say the least, slightly obnoxious to say more.

All men and women are born of woman, and I had a fifty-fifty chance of birthing a boy. But I had trouble grasping that very real possibility. That my female body could reproduce one that might be shaped so differently seemed incomprehensible to me. That I could reproduce vulva, clitoris, vagina, uterus — the equipment of a small woman — was reasonable to me, as reasonable as the mystical reproductive process can be. In my gut I could understand that a new person could be a woman person.

On the delivery table, with birth minutes away, after a tiring labor and more than an hour pushing my baby out, I very much wanted the birth process over, the drama complete. But even as the baby was coming out I feared, yes, feared, it would be a boy. The cold reality gripped me. The child could be a boy, not a girl, and I knew I would be disappointed. I had triumphed, with more than a little help from husband and hospital staff, over the threat of a medicated childbirth. I would have felt cheated, at the moment of birth, if my child

had been a boy. There is no doubt in my mind that I would
have loved that unborn boy baby, fallen in love with him as I
have with my daughter, but initially I would have been disappointed.

My preference for a daughter is a function of the times.
Women are saying, "It is our turn and our daughters' turn.
We want first-class status." If my first-born had been a son, I
know with certainty that I would try for a second child. I
would still want a girl, a daughter, to whom I can give the best
of me and the best of being female in a new era.

This desire for a girl is a strange mirror image of parental
hopes thirty years ago. Then it was better to have a boy. To
insure the name would be carried on. A big brother for the
second-born girl. Someone to take care of the little woman
and the little girl if something happened to Pa. What a reflec-
tion of the economic impotence of women! A son, a child, was
cast in the role of caretaker, provider, for the adult woman in
the event of tragedy. How ludicrous that a woman of thirty
years ago sighed with relief once she had a son, someone to
take care of her. She was not trained, nor was she encouraged
to develop a livelihood for herself. A boy infant was vested
with more power, and consequently more responsibility, than
his adult female parent.

No wonder parents wanted to create boys, creatures of
power and responsibility. Offspring with promising futures,
who would stand on their own, were preferred. How frustrating as a parent to produce only children who were female
and, by definition, powerless, destined to be frustrated and
live in some man's shadow. It was much easier to be powerful
if you were a man.

One militant feminist born first in a family of three
daughters describes the reaction to her youngest sister's birth
in the early 1950s this way: "People treated my mother as if
she'd given birth to a damaged child — like Sally was re-
tarded. They felt sorry for my mother since they assumed my
mother felt like a failure after trying three times and producing not one boy. Only my mother, in her sanity, thought
everyone else was nuts."

How different the public reaction when this woman had her own children in the early seventies. The initial time she felt her first baby kick was early on the morning of August 26, 1969. It was the anniversary of female suffrage, and women all over the country paraded and rallied, revivifying the fight for women's rights. That kick on that day was a sign, she hoped — a signal that the baby was a girl. Her friends and husband hoped so, too. They were right.

Pregnant again, three years later, she wanted a second girl. After all, she enjoyed a close relationship with her sisters. She wanted the same for her daughter. The father preferred another girl, too.

A friend of theirs who had delivered a wanted daughter a few months before practiced what she would say if a son were born to them. "A boy!" she would say to herself, trying to get a sincere lift into her voice. She couldn't say, "How wonderful. How lucky for you. Just what you wanted. How terrific. I bet you are thrilled." She knew they wouldn't be. The couple was delighted when a second daughter was born. Sighs of relief and cries of joy all around.

Another first-born daughter in a family of three girls consciously attempted sex selection before her first pregnancy. She wanted to conceive a daughter and had intercourse at the time she'd read was favorable to girls. Beth didn't even know if she was fertile, if she ever could conceive a child, but she so preferred a daughter over a son that she wanted to tilt the balance in favor of a girl.

Throughout her pregnancy, Beth talked kiddingly about the son growing inside her. Part of her was trying to get used to the idea of a boy. Another part of her was trying to ward off a boy fetus by talking about him.

Why did Beth want a girl? She says it is because there was never a boy child in her house. "I wouldn't know what to do with a boy; I know what to do with girls." She assumes, of course, that boys even as babies are something very different. "Besides," she confided, "my best relationships have been women — my mother, my sisters, my women friends." Beth's first child was a girl and she's about to conceive another child.

She doesn't want a son this time, either. She had picked out her daughter's name early and she has another girl's name lined up.

The parents of two daughters are, in some feminist circles, the modern-day success story. The parents of one girl are celebrated and considered lucky. The parents of a boy, or two boys, are pitied by some. Is the age of the woman truly upon us? Not yet. Are the parents of today who congratulate themselves for producing girls any different from the parents of yesterday who behaved the same way about boys? Is the river of prejudice turning from male to female? Will the third-born son in a family of no daughters be treated as a damaged child? Male privilege and male preference are ingrained enough in our culture that a son born third in a row of sons is not likely to suffer. However, in some segments of the feminist world the seeds of that kind of thinking are being sown.

What happens within the family, what happens to the parent-child relationship when the parents don't produce the preferred-sex child?

One pregnant woman told me within earshot of her three-year-old son that she had wanted him to be a girl and hoped her second born wouldn't disappoint her. The little boy overheard our conversation, since he was playing in the same room, very much aware of a new audience for his truck racing, doll playing, and furniture moving. His mother did not reach out to him for a snuggle as she spoke, and she did not reassure him that she loved him as a person. What exaggerated sibling rivalry will this boy suffer if the new baby turns out to be a girl?

One woman who wanted a daughter and was disappointed thinks her now school-age son wants to be a woman sometimes. "He'll pull his penis between his legs to make it look like a vagina. Then he'll ask me to look and say, 'See, I have a vagina like you.'"

Another woman who wanted a girl was pregnant and unmarried when she threw out the man who'd fathered her child. "When he was born and the doctor held him up in the palms of his hands, all I could see was *prick*. It looked enormous to me. When he was a tiny baby, on the changing table, I remember feeling that he was like, I don't know, a little *king*. Because of his penis, his maleness, he had a power over me. He intimidated me." Being the single parent of a girl would have been easier, she thinks. Now she worries about the need to bring strong and gentle men into the life of her child for him to emulate. She worries that every relationship her son has with a man is dependent upon that man's relationship with her. She feels she could have been her daughter's model, but with a son she has to go out looking.

One impressive woman explained how she has dealt with the issue of preferring a daughter to the son she has. "He knows we wanted a daughter. He knows why. Most certainly he knows we love him very much for himself." This couple has given their school-age son a thorough education in feminism, why there is a need for a women's movement, and how he can aid women's fight for equality and justice.

"We've explained to him how the bad men through the ages have hurt women, and at the same time hurt men by telling them what kind of men they should be. Our son knows he's in the vanguard of being a different kind of man."

This couple was up front with their son about their own prejudices, their own fears that raising a different kind of man in today's macho, sexist world would be harder than raising a different kind of woman. They admitted they were choosing the easier course. They admitted their own frailties and asked their son to accept them as they are — people struggling to overcome their own prejudices.

This young boy has an impressive grasp of history. He knows about the Pankhursts, Sappho, Michelangelo, Mozart, and the Amazons. He knows about the struggles people have had to endure.

Sometimes his resolve to be one of the vanguard, one of the "good men who help the women" weakens and he is wracked with tears and sobs that he's afraid he won't be strong enough. He fears the "bad men will get him." Is this pressure on a young boy too much? Are his parents doing him a disservice in asking him to be different? They are asking no more of him than society demands of other little boys who are wracked with fear that they won't measure up to a John Wayne standard, or a super-jock standard, of what it is to be a man. Is it better to demand a child measure up to a phony, tough, inhuman standard of what it is to be a *real man* in our culture, or is it better to ask a child to decide for himself just what kind of man he is going to be, and to encourage him to measure himself against his own standard, even if the pressures on him for being different may well be intense? Neither choice is easy, but the latter makes for a better person.

Preferring a child of one sex over the other sex is sexist. There is no other way to describe it. But it *is* human — a woman wanting a daughter, someone who is physically like her, with whom she will feel more physically comfortable. She wants a daughter to be her beneficiary, one to take on the feminist legacy for her own benefit and enrich it. She wants a child of the same sex so that she can re-experience all the bodily changes from infancy to childhood to adulthood. She wants a chance to watch the mysteries of maturation, this time perhaps with more wonder, but certainly with a lot less fear. She wants a chance to help ease that path toward maturity.

Fathers can talk with sons about chest hair, pubic hair, muscles rising, and testicles dropping. Mothers and daughters have underarm hair, pubic hair, breast development, and menstruation as topics for discussion. But, no matter how open, how sharing, how unfettered by psychological fears and complexes, no daughter can ask her father what it was like when he first got his period. No chance he's ever been there. Nor can a son ask his mother about her first erection and wet dream. Even the Platonic ideal of the non-sexist parent would have to draw the line at biology.

6

THE FEMINIST MOTHER

HE feminist woman of today was more than likely the pastel pink, beribboned, ruffled baby girl of decades past. The transformation from fragile baby to fiesty feminist, however, took more than the passage of time and a change of clothing from frilly to functional. At some point in the late nineteen-sixties or early seventies, each feminist woman — mother or not — reviewed her life. She assessed what parts of her life she had chosen, what she had controlled, and what had been dictated to her because of her sex.

Many struck out in anger at being brainwashed, sold a bill of goods. Some focused their anger and rage and jealousy on their brothers and fathers. Suddenly the smoldering rage was legitimized. Vague feelings were identified and named. Misogyny. Anti-feminism. All those years of conditioning had taken their toll.

One woman in her early forties described what her parents expected for her: "My parents drove me to school the first day of Radcliffe. We were parked in a diagonal space and my father introduced himself to the father in the next car. He said the classic thing. 'The only degree I want my daughter to get is an MRS.' I think he liked the idea I should have something to fall back on. My mother wanted me to be an educated person, but there was not a thought to a career, or working. I married a doctor, what could be better?

"I went to the graduate school of education," she continued, "because I thought it would be a safe thing. I sort of wanted to go to law school, but people said, 'Why, you are married and you will have a baby. Why go?' Some people had said I would never finish college because I was married. I didn't listen to them, but somehow I listened to the faceless, nameless people who put me off law school."

The majority of women of the last two decades were sent to school to mate. Parents told them they would meet a better kind of man while studying economics, or political science, or even Shakespeare — one liable to make more money. Women were told to work hard in high school and get into a good college, because the better the school, the higher caliber the future husband to be found. Too few were supported in developing real career goals, in setting sights on a professional star and charting a course in that direction. Supportive and secondary jobs were pushed by parents, counsellors, and teachers. The primary job was to find a husband and have children.

Like that Radcliffe graduate, large numbers of college women in the fifties and sixties were funneled, or directed themselves, into education. A woman could teach for a few years after college and maybe put her husband through graduate school or law school or medical school. In the sixties a woman could find a teaching job almost anywhere, wherever her man got into school or took a job. Teaching was always a good choice for a woman. She could "fall back on it in case something happened" — if he lost his job, if he died, if he ran away. At least a woman could teach, support herself and the kids, and still be back home at a decent hour to clean the house and get a good dinner on the table. The parents of these women, who had suffered joblessness during the Great Depression, wanted security for their children.

One woman named Carole was guided into elementary education by guidance counselors and by her own conditioned sense of what she could do to make a living. Even before she met the husband she was to support through seminary, Carole picked teaching because it was portable. Right after graduation she became engaged to David, and started teaching second grade. The first semester she hated — too many leggings put on and taken off; too many short words and finger-paint stains. She did not love building better minds within the elementary school system, but somebody had to pay the bills.

Throughout David's schooling Carole taught second grade and loathed it. After he started making money she returned to college. Carole had always loved science and math courses best. She wanted more of science than explaining the earth's rotation with a globe and flashlight to second graders. Now Carole works in a laboratory, does some taxidermy and enjoys the hours she spends making a living. She salvaged her dreams to some extent, but she probably will not make it to the top in scientific research. She's competing with people in the field who had a seven-year head start. She vows that for her six-year-old daughter career choice will be just that, a choice from a limitless list, not from a meager set of suitable female support occupations.

One woman who went to college in the sixties found she couldn't go back and salvage her dreams. Lynn entered college as a premedical student, planning to be a doctor. She'd apply to a good medical school, graduate, then practice. But at some point in her academically brilliant undergraduate career, she questioned what she was doing. Medical school was a long haul. Her family didn't have a lot of money. She couldn't expect a young husband to take a teaching job and put her through school. She took her doubts, along with her fine grades, to the college guidance counselor. Should she apply?

She came back from that session and ripped up the med school applications. The counselor had helped her see the light. After all, she could only expect to work as a doctor full time for a couple of years. She did want a family and children and she couldn't conceive of being an absentee mother. Then after the maternity leave, she'd probably only work part time.

The counselor pointed out that she would probably get into the medical school of her choice. But she would take the place of a male pre-med who would have a family to support someday. Was that really fair? She decided it was not. She deferred in favor of an unknown male premed student, whose grades and skills were probably inferior to hers. Was *that* really fair? Of course not.

Fortunately, in this generation Lynn wouldn't have been made to feel selfish about her dreams. The Lynn of today would be encouraged to develop herself, to be the best doctor she could be and not to defer her place in school, her place in a profession, her earned place in a higher income bracket to some unknown competitor — more equal, more deserving, and more responsible because he is male.

Women and mothers of today have come around to believing that it's great to be a woman. They want their daughters to feel positive about womanhood from the moment they are born. But some fear that their abundant praise of womanhood might have negative effects on their sons.

"I try so hard, maybe too hard, to reinforce how terrific it is to be a woman, because so many places Susan turns she gets a put down," said a mother of a girl and a boy. "When the Renee Richards story came out [a male physician and tennis player who underwent a sex-change operation to become a woman] I had to rethink what effect my pro-woman talk was having on my son. I decided the responsibility for a good male image is on Gene. That's his. I can rest easy."

Part of feeling positive about being a woman is enjoying and sharing pride in the female body. Occasionally the power of positive thinking becomes uterine chauvinism. One feminist mother explained the uterus to her three-year-old daughter as the place her new sibling was growing, a baby's house, and the place where her mother's magical monthly menstrual flow originated. Delighted to realize that she had a uterus, too, and that men do not, the three-year-old was heady with power. She had a uterus; her father did not. She could have a baby in her womb; her father could not. Prancing from room to room, and person to person, she chanted, "Papa doesn't have a womb! Papa doesn't have a womb!"

Most mothers of today were taught not to like their bodies. "Imagine a lioness not liking her body," suggests one feminist educator. The cultural lesson was well learned. Most women don't like their bodies, although individual parts are deemed passable. Secretions are powdered, sprayed, or washed away. Smells are masked. Hair is removed.

At some point in adolescence, most women took physical inventories of themselves. Often their mothers were there with an unwritten checklist of how their daughters stacked up against the ideal. Good legs, bad hips. Small waist. Small breasts. Neck too long. Teeth too crooked. Good eyes. That nose! After taking stock and giving advice and planning for orthodontia or plastic surgery, in the extreme, or dieting and camouflage dressing, at the least, the mothers of today learned what was wrong with them and how to fix it. They learned how to maximize the positive and snare a man. These same women swear they won't look at their daughters as if they were merchandise for sale. Then the daughters won't consider themselves irregulars, or seconds, or any quality of merchandise at all.

"When I was growing up I knew more about what was wrong with my looks, than what was right with them. How I looked, not what I did, was very important — particularly to my mother. I try not to care if my daughter wears clothes that don't match. It bothers me if she wears something that's awful, but I don't say a word to her. To myself I repeat, the clothes don't matter. She's three years old."

"We decided — I must have taken part in that decision — that my nose was bad. Big. Crooked. I had plastic surgery when I was a teenager, but the new nose was no good. About a year later I went in for another nose job. The second one was okay. They told me I'd never get married with the nose I'd grown."

What woman doesn't focus on her imperfections? The pamphlets distributed in health class in high school were among the sources that taught us how. "Aim to be average, so you can get a man," was the message. Remember the pictures showing who should wear what? Tall girls should wear horizontal stripes. Short girls should wear vertical ones. Both should end up looking either short enough or tall enough to date the guy in the second row. They never urged us to be tall and terrific. Be acceptable to him — that's what mattered.

"I'm trying to like my own body more now, so my daughter will model what she sees," said one mother. "I tell her that bodies of all shapes and sizes are beautiful and can feel good to be in. But I'm still very aware of my imperfections. I doubt if I hide that from her."

Even the loveliest and most competent of women are quick to point out their faults. The certainty that they are imperfect is so ingrained, so central to their sense of themselves, that very few of these women point to faults that can be corrected by diet or exercise or a change of hair color. They feel inadequate because, for example, "my legs are too short. Look, my knees are too low to the ground," or "my huge rib cage," "my tits are not wonderful," or "I'm shaped like a boy. I have no hips or ass. My shoulders are enormous." Each woman feels she is not quite woman enough. She wants her daughter to be able to accept herself as she is.

Many feminist mothers were never taught what to do with those bodies they don't like. Instead they were told what not to do. Don't let boys touch them. Don't touch the boys. They were told not to run and jump, not to turn cartwheels, because "your panties will show." "I was discouraged from using my body as a kid," remembers one mother of two girls, "so we've spent a lot of time encouraging Joy to be total body physical. Amy is more like that, more what we typify as masculine, naturally. We push Joy to literally jump in there. We encourage Amy to sit quietly and act in a small concentrated way. Mark and I have discussions about how far, how much we push the kids to be what they are really not."

"I show the kids how strong I am. Whenever there are tables to be moved, I pick one up and tell the kids that I am a strong woman moving furniture," reported one teacher. "They believe the media more than experience. Until they stop and think, they say that only men are strong. They forget that their mothers as well as fathers are strong enough to carry them."

"Growing up female had a lot to do with growing up afraid," says another teacher. "I know I was frightened of climbing up and jumping down. I'm still trying to undo some of those fears. I don't want that for the kids. The little girls say, 'I can't.' I say, how do you know till you try? Try. I can't whistle! I remember growing up and Mother saying, 'Girls don't whistle. Boys whistle.' I remember my friend Alison coming in one day and saying, 'I want to learn how to whistle. I know I'll be able to do it.' In a few days she was doing it, and teaching another girl how to do it. I try to undo that kind of crippling message."

That message in different variations crippled women into incompetence. Too many girls listened to their mamas say, "Girls don't" and they dutifully didn't. Female bodies weren't supposed to do carpentry, auto mechanics, electrical work, plumbing, or any other activity labeled masculine. Attempts at any "male" activity were often laughed at, disregarded, ridiculed, and certainly not taken seriously.

It is different now in some homes. One of these homes is Adelia's in Texas. Her political scientist father builds additions to the house in his non-professional hours, tinkers with electricity, and installs and repairs the pipes. For a while he was spending a lot of time under one of the family sinks. Eighteen-month-old Adelia was under there with him, wrenches in hand, apprenticing herself to her father. Adelia is being encouraged to consider plumbing as a vocation.

The same family scene would have been treated in an entirely different manner a few years ago. Adelia would have been "helping Daddy fix the sink," if she'd been allowed to stay in that dirty place at all. Today her parents talk about her taking on the plumbing job by herself at some time in the future. They know she won't be able to handle it for a few years, but they are letting her think about herself as someone who can use her body to fix things, and get paid for it.

Adelia and many other little girls of today are learning control of their bodies and control of their environment. They are learning, from the examples of their mothers and teachers and friends, that their own bodies are things of beauty and wonder and power. For too long women have not enjoyed the biological realities.

Pregnancy and birth have been endured, not celebrated. Is

this because the sex that can't be pregnant and give birth has been jealous? Pregnancy and birth are a physical test. Once a woman is pregnant and the fetus has grown to a certain size, whether the result is a miscarriage or a full-term baby, labor and delivery ensue. Labor is most often hours of hard physical work for the woman whose uterus rhythmically contracts to exert pounds of pressure on the baby she will deliver. After her cervix opens up to ten centimeters, she can push her child out. The baby moves down the vagina and the woman's body opens up to expel an entire human being! Her body stretches to many times its normal size, lets life out, then gradually resumes its original proportions.

For men there is no comparable physical experience. Do they feel jealous and left out? Do they downplay the value of the birth experience because they can't give birth? Multiple erections and ejaculations don't compare. Neither does weight lifting nor push-ups. Men have had to develop physical tests since they have been denied them biologically. They eat right, and exercise, and learn plays so they can bash into each other on the football field. They go into basic training for the armed services, slog through swamps, bayonet dummies, and push themselves to the extreme of physical endurance. They fight wars with the men of other nations, risk disease in jungles, suffer gunshot wounds, and sometimes die. Men have no biological test, as women have, so they must create proofs of courage, endurance, and strength.

Feminist mothers want their children — boys and girls — to enjoy their bodies. They want them to know their potentials and their strengths, and their joint participation in reproduction.

Feminist mothers generally resent the way they were prepared for motherhood and are educating their girl and boy children about parenthood more realistically. Heretofore women have not been trained to be mothers. Instead the culture, and the young mothers themselves, have relied upon maternal instinct to take over once the baby is on the scene. "Nobody told me it was normal to hate that screaming, demanding little creature once in a while. Mothers are all giving

— patient. I felt like a shit," admitted a mother of one child.

"I want my kids to know parenthood is not Kodak ads. Real motherhood is sitting on the john nursing the baby while you have diarrhea. There's nothing wrong with that. That is reality. But they don't show you that in the ads."

Women have not been trained for motherhood, but they've been blamed when they are not good mothers. "They blame it on penis envy," said one educator, "or that your relationship with your own mother was conflicted. At the San Diego Zoo they had to teach a gorilla how to be a mother by showing her films." A human mother doesn't get lessons.

She does get an on-the-job, continuous series of do's and don'ts from the people around her, however. When she is trying to be a different kind of mother, and her family is teaching her to be the traditional kind, conflict, pain, and anger result. "It's a struggle for me," admitted one mother. "I try to set a good example for my daughter — to be a magical mother who makes caramel apples and at the same time is committed to my work. But there are terrible inequities. Every once in a while my husband goes away on business trips for three or four days. He gets a lot of sympathy. 'Poor Herb has to be away from his wife and family.' When I was away on business recently the reaction was the same, 'Poor Herb and Jenny, the wife and mother has run out on them.' The family message is that women shouldn't travel on business. A social absence a couple of months ago was fine, but to be away to work is bad.

"Herb and I know we are both entitled to business trips, regardless of sex, but the outside criticism hurts me. When I got home all I heard was how Jenny missed me, how she cried and didn't sleep through the night. The realities were distorted by my in-laws to make me feel guilty. It is hard enough being a different sort of mother without sabotage from the extended family."

"They ask me outright, and sometimes just with their eyes, what kind of mother am I," says a mother of a small boy. "I know the parenting I am doing is fine. I have to work. I want to work. Until I was five I was my mother's whole world. It

or me, but I can't repeat that devotion. Some-
if I should.

had a very exciting opportunity — to work in
school developing new curriculum and doing
rogressive work with disadvantaged high school
only offered me a full-time job, which would have
more than full-time. I had to say no, because of
Nic̲h̲o̲ and because of me. I had to miss it and don't know
when that kind of opportunity will come again. Once again,
the mother has to compromise."

One couple devised a solution without female compromise,
but not without struggle. "When I has home I was very dis-
satisfied. I depended on Mark for all my adult company. I
didn't enjoy being that many hours with children — it was not
that interesting to me. I missed working, like my mother. But
she went so far as to say she wished she never had children!
That was hard for me to take. So when Mark suggested I go
back to work full time, it was like my first marriage when my
husband went back to school. I was afraid it would be a rerun
of an exploitative situation. We were able to talk about the
way I was feeling, but I had no confidence that he could cope
with our child. I had to develop confidence in him. We do
things differently, which still presents problems. That's not a
sexist issue — just two persons with ideas about raising kids,
two people making decisions."

Many feminist mothers admitted to fighting an inbred
sense of contempt for men before they could proceed with
any kind of co-parenting. They also spoke about men being
incompetent. "I always thought they were dumb and naturally inept around children." "I go into the kitchen and I take
over, so I have to stay out. He hasn't had much experience
cooking. He's had such frustrating experiences. When it said
'fold in the egg whites,' he folded and folded and folded, and
they died. A dozen eggs!"

"I've had to let him make mistakes, or wait until he remembers what clothes he forgot to pack for the baby. Sure, I'm
tempted to jump in, take over, mother him and the baby, but
I fight it. I don't want to be in charge forever. Michael has a

lot of learning to do. I'm impatient," says the mother of a six-month-old.

To this point in history women have been the caretakers of the physical needs of men and of children. Part of their job has been to inculcate the younger generation in the ways of the culture — to turn their sons and daughters over to the patriarchal system. They have been traitors to their daughters. Today's feminist mother was more than likely raised by a naive traitor, one who may still address the envelopes Mrs. John Smith. The younger woman must face the painful fact that her own mother reinforced the cultural limitations placed on women. She must deprogram herself, and fight the reflex to repeat the pattern.

"I don't let on to the children that they have the option not to work. For too many women, struggling with the choice has robbed them of the energy to succeed. Women work, that's it. Mothers work, a fact. People work," said a mother and daycare teacher. Mothers who themselves still feel guilty or uneasy about reconciling working and motherhood want to spare their own children the pain.

"In years past the women who made it were seen as deviants," explained Dr. Carol Nadelson, a psychiatrist who is the director of medical student education at Boston's Beth Israel Hospital and an Associate Professor at Harvard Medical School. "They accepted that title. It is very hard if you are a so-called normal person to accept that label. Harder still when you are a kid." But more "normal" women are making it, and as parents point out their successes children will learn that they can win without jeopardizing their femininity or masculinity.

Among the women I spoke with — mothers, educators, mental health professionals — I found an interesting correlation between attitude and age. The women fifty and over seemed, by and large, much less disturbed by sexism. Many of these women are successful — they've won in life. Are they less agitated because their childraising, non-sexist or sexist, is done? Are they content to live in a world that is familiar, even if it is a sexist world? Many of these women were reluctant to admit sexism had hampered them in any way whatsoever. Few complained of discrimination in their professional lives. How can that be explained? Denial? Disremembering? These older women who succeeded in a male world somehow found personal formulae for success. If these women condemned and vowed to change a system that had rewarded them, were they not criticizing themselves? Does age explain the disparity in feelings about sexism and childraising? Have older women removed themselves from the whole feminist fight?

Many mothers speak of helping their children, more often their daughters, chart the path to a career goal. "I tell her she can't be a ballerina and a dentist. She will have to choose, because preparation for both are rigorous. She can't have it all, no one can, and the sooner she learns that choice excludes some options, the better chance she will have of making it."

"I've told them, do what it takes to become what you want to become," says a teacher, mother of four girls and a boy. "I've become what I wanted to; I think I'm a good model for them. One daughter has loved airplanes since she was tiny and wants to be an aeronautical engineer or a pilot. *If* that is what she wants, then she has to prepare herself. Take the right courses, maybe go into the service, and if they offer a special training program in the service, take it. I encourage them to figure out what they want, and how to get it."

Says one writer, "I tell my daughter every grownup has to earn money, so figure out how you are going to do it."

"I encourage all the kids to broaden their options," offers a high school administrator and mother of four. "Try law school. Try business school. While you still have the time, see, try, experiment in the areas that mean something to you when you are still young enough to try."

Feminist mothers are fighting, within themselves and for their children, the indoctrinated ideal that a woman should lead a protected life under the aegis of a man. The fantasy persists despite the fact that more than half the women in this country with children under the age of six are workers. So many were raised to live a lifetime of protected childhood, never realizing that "every grownup has to earn money." "I wish somebody had told me I'd have to support myself for the rest of my life," moaned one teacher.

While feminist mothers and fathers are preparing their children for specific careers and goals, they often disagree over whether or not part of that preparation should be an education about sexism. Strangely, parents who were discriminated against because of sex often believe their own children will magically escape sexism.

When asked to explain how their daughters would be exempt from sex prejudice, parents were at a loss. "She has a good, loving relationship with us. That will carry her through," was heard often. "We're not sexist," was another explanation. But the world is.

Should feminist mothers tell their children that sexism is out there? Or should they let them find it out by themselves? "I didn't talk sexism to the kids. I didn't say, 'You are going to have a tough time because you are girls.' Like I didn't say, 'You are going to be discriminated against because you are black.' They will find those things out," says one Portland, Oregon, mother.

"I don't preach to the kids. I don't want them to reject the ideas because they are mine. Last night, my daughter who is a frosh at the University of Michigan said, 'You are right. There is no comparison. My two female professors are so much better. It proves to me the women have had to be so much more super to get to the same level as the men.' "

"When she is ready for the notion of sexism, or racism, we will address it. She will observe and ask. Strident feminists, non-racists, or whatever are harsh in their advocacy. It is not a positive thing around young kids. What good does it do to tell a child many times a day that women are oppressed? I don't think it has any meaning to a child of four, and it becomes offensive to other people. She will end up forming her own concepts. The issues she chooses to fight or embrace may not be our issues. She may not be interested in fighting the feminist issue. Certainly, if we try to make feminism an issue for her, it won't be, I'll bet. Some day she will probably come home and announce she is a feminist, as if I had never heard the word," says one mother.

But one East Coast mother feels the opposite. "I'm going to have to tell my daughter about sexism. The thought of that conversation makes me want to throw up. She is going to take shit because she is a female. I hate it, but I know it. To send her out to architectural school, for example, without warning her first about what might happen would be criminal. What do you do, wait for your child to be knifed before teaching her how to defend herself? Not me. Can I help her become a realist without turning her into a cynic? I don't know."

Other women adopt a historical perspective. "You must educate the children, boys and girls, about history. About what the 'bad' men have done to women. Go to history and literature, and show the child who has been different and who has triumphed. Chopin, daVinci, Keats, Chatterton, the suffragists, etc."

Is sexism like sex used to be? Something dirty, to be ignored? Is the fight against sexism something a child should pick up on the street or learn at home? Is feminism best learned by osmosis or through structured study?

One California librarian feels she has already lost the sexism battle with her two young children. This woman has made a career out of feminism — she edits a bibliography of non-sexist children's books. But her professional beliefs aren't translated to her childraising. "Ironically, I'm set with two very sex-stereotyped kids. My daughter wants no more than a lace dress and fancy scarf to thrill her. My son loves trucks. I did an experiment with my two-year-old son. I put him down in the middle of an aisle of a toy store. Snap, he was over at the trucks and cars. The dolls were ignored."

However, this librarian and other mothers are hopeful that they will be fine examples for their girls and boys — the kind of woman their children can look up to. The girls can hope to be like her. The boys can hope to mate with someone like her. She is neither slave, nor martyr, nor weak. She is smart and capable and strong.

Arlene fears that her children will grow up "in a very confused way because Frank and I share everything. He doesn't say, 'that's not my work.' He picks up the crumbs with the vacuum. I wash dishes. He washes dishes. A friend's father says, 'I'm not going to vacuum. I'm no schmuck. Your daddy vacuums, he does laundry.' After hearing that a while I hope they will say, So what! More fathers are doing that now."

"The burden of modeling behavior falls on mothers, but the burden of discussing the issues falls on fathers," decided one high school guidance counselor. "If the old man is willing to share the society-given power with his wife, that says more than if I stand there and rail. I'm getting my Ph.D. now. My daughter is intrigued with the idea of having two doctors in the family — one a woman. I'm very clear about my being a model for her.

"When I started to go off to do workshops and give speeches, the kids were confused. Fathers are famous and travel. Mothers stay at home.

"At home we try to deprogram by modeling. In the early days of feminism I was into having it both ways — wanting to be professionally equal, but in day-to-day relationships expecting him to come to my rescue. In exchange for his doing half the housework and child care, he has required that I not play both ends against the middle — that I fix my own damn car and learn to fix the vacuum. It takes two people dedicated to make it work. Changing fuses, putting together a box-top toy, if I sit down for a moment I can do it. Immediately, I want to give up."

The majority of feminist mothers agree they should treat children as children, and not as boys and girls. At the same time they are very conscious of the various pressures exerted on boys and girls that mold them into preset patterns. The women feel they shouldn't act one way with girls, another with boys. They should, because of their fair-minded politics, view all children the same. Some do not

"I want to know what a little boy is like. Yes, I'd like to round out the set. If there is no difference between our daughter and a son we might have, let me see it for myself," one mother offered. Another wants to experience the sexual chemistry with a little boy. "I want that all-out love my daughter feels for her daddy."

"I keep telling myself, I'm a *parent* to a *child,* not that I'm a mother to a daughter. The sooner we erase those classifications, the better it will be," said another parent.

One mother made a painful comparison between her experiences as mother to a boy and mother to a girl. "Boys are much easier. Your own psychic shit doesn't get in the way. I think the mother-daughter relationship is very troubled. It sent me into therapy. I was seeing four generations of mothers rejecting daughters. My grandmother, mother, me, and my daughter. Each one different from the preceding generation and rejected by the mother. I wasn't going to sit and watch it happen to me.

"It is very difficult for an aggressive woman to come through this society with her femininity intact, without some kind of therapeutic intervention or some kind of terrific mother to screen out society.

"I allow, even encourage, if I am honest, a degree of dependency on the part of my daughter that I deny my sons. I have some guilty feelings about not being with her that I don't have about my sons. The expectations of a mother-daughter relationship are so high. The boob tube tells us that mothers and daughters toil in the kitchen together. For me and most women there is a gap between what your head tells you and your gut tells you.

"Even though I know that parenting has to be evaluated qualitatively, not quantitatively, I know my daughter sees less of me than other girls see their mothers, and I still feel guilty."

These mothers cannot help but feel some guilt. Years of conditioning and peer pressure are difficult to ignore. It is important that they receive as much support as possible in their effort to raise non-sexist children — especially support from the fathers.

7

THE FEMINIST FATHER

HE challenge and more than half the responsibility for raising non-sexist children within the confines of the nuclear family lies with today's adult men. Despite the strictures placed on men to be strong, unfeeling, responsible males that have often left them alienated from love and obsessed by work, and despite the other negative fallout men have suffered in the form of ulcers and heart attacks, they do have power. They make more money than women; women make 57 percent of what men make. A male high-school graduate in 1974 averaged $12,000 a year, while a woman college graduate averaged only $9,000. Men hold more elective offices. On Capitol Hill, the peak year for women holding elective congressional offices was 1962 when twenty women served, making up 5 percent of the membership. It clearly is a man's world, and he is reluctant to give up the privileges.

Both Warren Farrell in his book, *The Liberated Man,* and Marc Feigen Fasteau in his book, *The Male Machine,* decry the pressures on men in our society. They call for men's liberation. That's great, but let men work for it, not women. Men have had advantages while they've been enslaved that women have never enjoyed. Comparing men's oppression to women's oppression is like comparing the minimum-security federal prison at Allenwood, Pennsylvania, to Attica.

Because it clearly is a man's world, much of the power to effectively raise non-sexist children to take over that world lies with men. Somehow they must be made to share both the power and the daily responsibilities of childraising.

In the course of interviewing families for this project, I met a very different breed of men — men who are soft and strong, funny and bright and nurturing, who have chosen to define their own lives instead of letting the culture dictate to them. How did they get that way? Through intense introspection about themselves as males? After confrontation and challenge by the women in their lives? Could it be magic?

One father, who is the primary parent for his two girls, says, "My mother gave me an enormous sense of fairness and justice. That is what I want to pass on. Early photos of our family show me posed with a doll in my arms. My brother, too. I must have been eight or nine and those pictures say a lot about the way I was brought up. I must have chosen that doll, maybe a favorite doll, to be part of a family picture for the album . . . When I was a child I hated to hear anyone laugh at a child, or say, 'Isn't that cute.' I don't think I took any abuse for that sensitivity. I didn't take much abuse from anybody for anything." Today Joe remains sensitive to young children. He's chosen early-childhood education as his profession.

How did this father decide to work part time, stay with the children, and encourage his wife to work full time? "That first year of Joy's life, when I was working full time, every time Joy cried in the night, or her diaper needed changing, Ellie would always beat me to her. She didn't even know it. The only way I could get to see to some of Joy's needs was to say, 'Go sit down.' "

Joe decided he wanted to play a part in his child's life in contrast to that which his own father played in his early life. "My father remembers almost nothing about our early life. A few flashes here and there, but not much. He remembers our trips together as a family. My mother always wanted to stop, have a meal on the road, but he always had to get there, had to average sixty miles an hour, no matter what. Now he admits he was in too much of a hurry. He had to get us wherever we were going. He realizes now he missed it. Sad. I have no doubt that I am spending my time now the way I want. I will never regret the time with the kids."

Like Joe, Eric also wanted to be a part of family life in a big way. "In 1970 when our daughter was born I knew that for me parenting was something I would be involved in. Non-sexist childraising, at that point, was not a big goal. So when she was born, I was working in film, would work very hard for a couple of days, then have time off. When I worked full time after our son was born, it was tough. I would put in three hours with the kids in the morning before I went to work. Then after work I took our daughter, and Vicki took the baby."

Parents who share their child-care responsibilities equally have often picked professions with parenthood in mind. Academics, film makers, writers, photographers, and free-lance workers of many sorts can more easily structure making a living around parenthood, than can anyone with a nine to five job.

"My father had to work sixty hours a week. Even if he had wanted in his head to spend time with his kids, he couldn't. When you are sixty-five you have the opportunity, but there is no basis for that kind of a relationship with a child. It slipped by. I know I sought out the kind of work I've done, because I wouldn't get locked into a time when work became the most important thing, my whole life. I wanted to spend time with my kids, especially when they were in the first three years. I think that's where you start with kids to build. You can't say, 'I don't have the time now, I'll do it later.' There are no models for me, and that's a problem — not my parents or any other adults I knew, or even friends of ours. Now our friends feel envy about the relationship I have with our two."

Joe, Eric, and others like them have sought access to daily life with their children and have learned the skills and chores of parenting. But the important factor is that they wanted, preferred, and chose an active life as parents. No amount of ordering and lecturing forced them into that role — at least there was no pressure from society as we know it. The pressure to change must come from within each man — until women can wrest half the power from men and force them to share the responsibilities of child care.

Selma Greenberg, feminist educator, thinks men will come

around only after they are forced out in the cold. Speaking at the Women's Action Alliance conference on Non-sexist Early Childhood Education, Greenberg said, "For ages women have been setting up men to be loved, in exchange for bed and board and protection. When women board and protect themselves and no longer do the emotional part for daddy, men will have to earn that love themselves."

As developing children we learn about ourselves from the people around us. Girl children learn about themselves from their mothers *and* their fathers. If a male parent values a child enough to spend time and energy seeing to her daily needs, then the child will value herself. His worth as a thing of power and respect in the world will rub off on her. At an early age children figure out that men are often considered more valuable than women.

Marjorie Lozoff of the Wright Institute in Berkeley, California, discovered that self-determination in female students was closely tied to a satisfying relationship between father and daughter. In the November 1975 issue of *Family Circle,* Lozoff claimed that when "fathers treated their daughters as interesting people, worthy of respect and encouragement, the young women got the idea that their femininity was not endangered by the full development of their talents."

Many successful women credit their atypical fathers for fostering their careers and for allowing them to be atypical individuals growing up. Caryl Rivers, writing in *The New York Times Magazine,* credits her father for directing her toward feminism as she grew up in the 1950s. She noticed that her father was more intimately involved in her world than were the fathers of her friends involved in theirs. Rivers' dad even doubled as her basketball coach when she started playing Catholic Youth Organization basketball. Thanks to him, she was the only girl who could execute an "unladylike" jump shot and be an aggressive, winning basketball player.

When Rivers started dating, she wanted to hide her basketball trophies, "sure that my boyfriends would think me an Amazon with huge thighs, but my father argued that I had won them, and they ought to stay." He was telling her she could be strong and a successful athlete, which was not antithetical to being attractive, datable, or womanly.

Rivers says she married a man like her father, who today tells their daughter, " 'Girls can be anything they want.' He will transmit to her the message my father (and my mother) beamed to me: You are a person of worth, of value, and it is your right to achieve and grow." The importance of men who have broken through stereotypes is obvious to Rivers, who writes, "If I am a free woman, and I believe I am, it is due in no small measure to the fact that I have lived with — and loved and been nurtured by — free men."

Gail Sheehy in her book *Passages* examines the mentor syndrome. Often a successful woman has attached herself early in her working life to a very successful man, who has served as a nurturing papa of sorts. He has reinforced her sense of worth and has taught her skills to use as she deals with success.

Children brought up in families with liberated men grow up with a living example of what it is to be a complete person. Conversely, families where the fathers refuse to participate in daily child and house care set back the cause of non-sexism greatly.

Take a look at Louise and Tom and their two daughters. His politics are right — equal pay for equal work, respect for women on the job, a belief in the value and worth of female human beings. He loves his daughters and is glad they had girls. But Tom doesn't want to have anything to do with the daily, or even weekly, care of his children other than the bounce-on-the-knee-before-bedtime routine. Louise works part time in a career she enjoys, but has not even part-time help at home from Tom. The laundry, food, apple-juice pouring, floor wiping, and child bathing are all up to her. She hates the loneliness of the job and is beginning to hate him.

Louise talks feminism to her kids, and she functions like a superwoman — an angry superwoman. As he is, Tom is a negative factor in that house. Despite hearing declarations of equality, the children see gross inequality. From Tom's behavior they are learning that men leave the housework to women, that they sit and read and smoke and watch television, and that they very seldom care for children.

Louise wonders if the house might be a more positive place for the children with Tom gone. "I can talk till I'm blue in the face, but if Tom never does these things I tell the children men *and* women do, they just won't believe it." If Tom's behavior doesn't change, their daughters, despite the information they are being fed about equality of the sexes, will grow up believing all men are like the one they saw in their living room. They will not expect their husbands or lovers to behave any differently. They will assume, alone, the burdens of house and children and job.

One mother credits her modeling and her husband's modeling for proving to her child that adult life can be shared. "I'm raising my daughter so she won't grow up and have her mind cluttered with all the minutiae of life. It takes energy every day to worry about whether there's enough half-and-half for the coffee or clean underpants for the family. She'll expect someone to share the shit work. And she'll find him."

Are the men who are active in raising non-sexist children the wave of the future? Are the men who are reassessing themselves and their behavior in terms of the new desires and demands of women growing in number? I think so. One reason may be that the climate is more favorable for males to learn nurturing behavior in childhood today. Still, boys in traditional homes do their practicing with dolls behind closed doors.

In the beginning of his parenting, my husband, Jeff, didn't know how to do any child-care tasks. He never practiced on a doll. He didn't have the Charlotte Zolotow book *William's Doll* as a part of his life. The story is a current one about a little boy who wants a doll despite the objections of his father and brothers. Luckily for William, his grandmother understands and explains to his father that William needs a doll to practice on so when he's a father he'll know what to do.

Another participatory father, who cares for his son half

the time, took a lot of abuse from acquaintances and family about his desire to nurture his child: "They think it's funny, weird, that I am so involved with the baby. They make cracks like, 'When are you going to grow tits?' They're trying to make fun of me, saying I'm like a woman. Damn it, I'd like to grow tits. When it comes to sustaining the life of this child, I *am* inadequate."

Men raised by these feminist fathers will be different. The boy children will have a close emotional and physical relationship with their fathers. In most of our society the only excuse men have to touch each other is in the context of sports — the football huddle, men in a tight circle, arms wrapped around each other's shoulders, the rear-end slap that sends the team into play. One set of team members slap each other in encouragement to sock, tackle, and top the other team. Padded gloves worn by hockey players restrict their sense of touch. In the more naked sport of basketball, touching is not allowed. The whistle blows. It is time out.

In this homophobic world, men aren't supposed to touch unless they are locked into a sports battle, bonded by grief, or brought together by the bottle. After a death, men can sob into each other's arms, but only if the crying is brief and followed by a gruff "I don't know what came over me" apology. Drunken men can carry each other home. That's about all the touching grown men in our society are allowed to do without someone raising an eyebrow and questioning the man's sexual preference.

The rules have been somewhat looser between fathers and sons. Dads are allowed to snuggle baby boys and throw them in the air, but very soon the boy child is labeled a man and set apart from any physical gentleness from his father. The story of one father during the Second World War illustrates this. When his son was three this father decided he should no longer kiss the child before he went to bed. No more kissing. No more hugging. A firm warm handshake was indicated by the boy's age and, more importantly, by his sex. Certainly the father's hesitation to be physically close with a small manperson was more an imitation of what he had seen in his own family, than any subconscious fear of homosexuality. But for whatever reason, he acted in the belief that males were not supposed to touch, even if one were a child of three and the other a father in his early forties.

It is not surprising that many of today's new fathers in feminist families want a girl to be their first-born child. Some were themselves born princes, heir to all things good and powerful and beneficial within their families, while their sisters often got the second cut, the leftovers, because they were girls. As expectant fathers they seek retribution for their sisters and expiation of their own guilt formed by the sibling-rivalry game in which they had had an unfair advantage. Some expectant fathers want girls because they genuinely believe women are better than men.

Occasionally expectant fathers who want girls anticipate that they will know how to be a new kind of father — a feminist father — to a girl, but don't know how to be a new kind of father to a boy. They don't know what this new era of feminism demands of male adults and male children.

When they were growing up, they were taught that man was strong, victorious, right, successful, and a host of other qualities that are impossible for any human being to sustain. A father was encouraged to teach his son that real manhood was synonymous with those superlatives. Knowing in his own heart that he fell miserably short of the ideal, he had to set an example for his son to model. How could he do it? For one, he could lie and pretend he was the perfect man. He could strengthen his son by pointing out the boy's weaknesses. He could discourage unmanly behavior. Whatever the technique, if the father himself felt weak and unmanly inside, he hid that from his son. He genuinely wanted his son to be better than he was — more of a man.

One father admitted he felt lucky having a girl as his first child in the early 1970s. All the articles and books pouring out with the rebirth of feminism guided him in being a better father to a baby girl. He felt he could teach her all the good things society had let him capitalize on because he was a man. He'd share with a girl child all of the male secrets. With his help, the doors would open for her. When he considered what it would be like to be the father of a boy in the early seventies, he was thrown into a quandary. Take away the trucks? Make most certain that any toy guns that came into the house were disposed of? Refuse to let him develop into a male chauvinist pig?

What a reversal of the *Carousel* lyric was this father-to-be. Unlike Billy Bigelow, this man felt he could have fun with a daughter, but he'd have to be a FATHER to a son. He learned a lot about himself and about babies from his daughter. Loving and snuggling and playing with her and tending to her needs, he learned a great deal about what it is to be a parent. Because she was a girl, he suspects, he could relax and relate to her as grownup to baby. Not worrying about what kind of man, what kind of FATHER he was being to a son, he took his cues from her personality and from his own. When the couple's son was born four years later, he was able to forget about man/man, father/son, and able to remember parent/baby.

Single fathers have an advantage in the area of redefining what it is to be a man. Choosing single parenthood in some cases, having it thrust upon them in others, single fathers have to be both mother and father to their children. When a terrified and insecure little boy needs holding and stroking and reassurance in the middle of a long night, there is no space for a loving father to ask, "Is this manly?" If the mother used to fulfill that "womanly, motherly" function, but the mother is gone and the child is hurting, a loving father fills the need. He is soft and warm, speaks low, and banishes the nightmare or explains a painful reality. A loving father will fulfill the child's needs first and worry about his male image later.

"I had to be mother and father to my children. Up until the time my wife left, I guess I thought mother and father were different. Now I must do what two parents used to do. Their mother is a continent away. Being alone with my kids has stretched me as a man — not just the survival skills I've had to master, but my attitude. Things had to be done, so I did them."

This father says he is physically close with his children and that he has broken through the DON'T TOUCH barrier usually erected between father and child. "I massage my son and daughter. Massage really relaxes me, and we sort of fell into it as a family. I knead the tension out of both my kids; it's soothing to them and to me. We enjoy each other's touch."

The son's best friend is a girl, but for a long time the two friends would not walk home together after school. The derision, the teasing from their classmates, was too much. Each would find her/his way to their after-school meeting place alone. One afternoon Daniel asked his father if he could sleep over at Monica's house. Mad telephoning ensued between the father of Daniel and the mother of Monica about the etiquette of such a sleep-over party. What do they wear? Where do they sleep? How late do they stay up? Dare we do it? She's a girl. He's a boy. God knows what might happen.

With saneness operating in full force, the parents looked at the facts. The kids are ten years old. They are kids. The real fun of a sleep-over party is sleeping in the same room (living room or bedroom, it doesn't seem to matter), staying up late, eating junk food, giggling, and whispering. Okay, the sleep-over party had a go-ahead, but not before her mother and his father did a lot of hard thinking. Were they warping their kids' future sex lives by allowing this kind of intimacy? Were they cretins if they said "No, boys and girls do not have sleep-over parties, and don't ask why." The sleep-over party was a great success — much late night giggling and confidence sharing and junk-food eating. They even had a lovely breakfast the next morning.

The mother of the girl called the father of the boy to report on the events. She related to the father what she called an amazing happening. "At breakfast, Monica reached over and stroked Daniel." A gentle tap really, she explained — the kind of touch that reinforces a point of conversation, a sort of "I like you" touch. "Daniel didn't flinch," the mother went on. "Monica's father hates to be touched. He will not allow it. But Daniel thought nothing of it. It was as if Monica said, 'Hi.' "

No surprise to the father of Daniel. "I massage my son. I touch him. He's used to being touched by his father and he enjoys it. We are men who touch. Why should he flinch?"

Other single fathers with whom I spoke acknowledged that when they volunteered to assume custody of their children when their marriages disintegrated, they had little idea of what twenty-four-hour-a-day care really meant.

One father whose wife left to establish her own life when the daughters were three and not quite two admitted single parenthood was a rude awakening. He was angry with himself for the life skills he had never developed, but had depended upon women to provide. He was determined to provide his two toddlers with skills so they would be independent.

For a while, after his wife left and he was between jobs, this father applied for public assistance to help him through the critical period. The experience was dreadful. While women with two toddlers were not questioned as closely about their motives, he felt he was under the utmost scrutiny for choosing to stay home with his two little girls rather than leave them during the day and take on a full-time job. "What kind of man are you?" they asked. To the social workers, father love seemed a much less valuable commodity than mother love. The experience radicalized this single father more than his wife's leaving had.

He stayed home with his girls for eight months. By that time they were adjusted to life with a father, and he was adjusted to the demands of single parenthood. His child-care and house-care skills were honed and he was ready to take on a job and be a working father.

As the father of two daughters in the mid-1970s, this man has been committed to opening as many doors for them as possible. Functioning as a single parent has made him realize that women's liberation is men's liberation, too. He felt incompetent when his wife left. Now he vows, "It will be different for my daughters, and their husbands." He is more competent now, he says, "and more attuned to the children. There's no other adult here." He hopes the girls will grow up liberated. "If my wife had been raised in a less sexist time, maybe she would never have had to leave." He still hopes she'll be able to come back.

Some single fathers labor under the threat of becoming super-dads. For too long feminist working mothers aspired to super-mom status, that rank of capable, smart, all-things-to-all-members-of-the-family women. Super-mom did it all herself and periodically collapsed with exhaustion. Strange liberated echoes of an old Anacin television ad — "I'd rather do it myself!" Super-dads are a slightly different breed. They are defiantly proving to their old selves how terrific and competent and self-sufficient their new selves are.

Take for example Tom, father of one toddler still in the equipment stage of life — that stage when you cannot leave the house without at least one diaper and one change of bottoms, a full bottle of something that will not spoil, a toy, and a stroller. When Tom was first alone with his son, he congratulated himself when he got out the door fully equipped. Then as he gained confidence, and packing the stroller bag became a habit, Tom developed a real pride about his skills.

"People treat men alone with children very differently from the way they treat women. Every biddy treats me like a bungler — like I don't know what I'm doing. Now I know what I'm doing and I resent their advice. They are condescending, waiting for me to make a mistake. It's assumed women know what they are doing and the men do not."

For a while Tom strove to prove the biddies, and whoever else was watching, wrong. He became a super-dad. Laden with toddler in one arm, folded stroller over the other arm, and his body draped with a package or two, he scorned people who tried to help him navigate in and out of doors. Perhaps Tom had to prove he could do it all himself. Before long, he saw the error of his ways. Instead of resenting it now, Tom is quick to take advantage of the fact that men with children get help more easily on the street. It is sexist, he agrees, but he is willing to exploit that prejudice. "I'm a single parent with a full-time job. I'm tired. I'll take all the help I can get."

8

"THESE KIDS TODAY"

eVERY child is color coded at birth. Its name is typed on a pink-for-girl, blue-for-boy card that is placed at the head of the hospital bassinet. It is wrapped in a pink or blue blanket in the nursery lest an observer forget it is a girl or a boy, and mistake it for a baby.

All babies are born the same color — a blue-gray translucence. Only with the first breath does each baby change from blue-gray to black or white or brown or yellow. All children come out equal, but quickly race is noted, sex is checked, and the world begins the process of imprinting on that baby what it wants from a brown girl, a black boy, a white girl, a yellow boy. The expectations vary for each race, sex, and social class.

"The little boy screams leaving his mother's womb and in the delivery room they say, 'He's all boy,'" observed Dr. Robert E. Gould. "The girl screams and yells and they ignore it till she smiles and then they say, 'Isn't she pretty? She'll be a heart-breaker when she grows up.' Early on they learn what is approved, what is not approved. It starts from day one. A little boy is born, you throw it up in the air, catch it. Nobody would throw a little girl baby, she's too fragile. What a difference in the way you handle the babies at the age of one day. Long before they understand the language, they understand the non-verbal communication."

One active feminist experimented with her newborn. As she wheeled the baby in the carriage she would tell some passersby that the baby was a boy. "My, he looks strong," they would remark and take a swipe at "his" arm. When she said that the baby was a girl, "she" would be patted, stroked, and told "she" was pretty. The mother had proof positive, right in her own neighborhood, of how differently boys and girls are treated. One day the baby could tolerate swipes, another day the same baby could only endure a soft pat. Strength and sex-role behavior are only in the eye of the beholder.

A baby's sex is all important. Few hospitals are radical enough to wrap all babies in yellow or type BABY CARMICHAEL on the identifying card. In 1977 we are still stuck in the girl/ boy rut. The first question anyone asks after a birth is, "What is it?" The questioner is asking the sex with an assumption that when the sex of a child is known a great deal about that child has been revealed.

Lois Gould wrote a fanciful story about a child whose sex was hidden from all except itself and its parents. *X: A Fabulous Child's Story* tells the tale of a special experiment to raise an X, a child, not a boy or a girl. Adults in the story were confounded and embarrassed by an X. They knew the appropriate toys and clothing to give girls and boys, but what did you give an X? Even X's schoolmates were at first disturbed and later radicalized by X's freedom to basket weave and shoot baskets, to race and bake.

The parents at X's school were disturbed by X's disruptive influence. Girls were not acting like girls, boys were not acting like boys. The parents feared dire consequences and labeled X "Problem Number One." So X underwent a psychiatric examination and, no surprise to non-sexists, passed with flying colors. The psychiatrist reported, " 'In my opinion, young X here . . . is just about the *least* mixed-up child I've ever Xamined! . . . X has absolutely no identity problem! X isn't one bit mixed up! As for being a misfit — ridiculous! X knows perfectly well what it is! Don't you, X?' The doctor winked. X winked back.

" 'But what *is* X?' shrieked Peggy and Joe's parents. 'We still want to know what it is!'

" ' 'Ah, yes,' said the doctor, winking again. 'Well, don't worry. You'll all know one of these days. And you won't need me to tell you.'

" 'What? What does he mean?' some of the parents grumbled suspiciously.

"Susie and Peggy and Joe all answered at once. 'He means that by the time X's sex matters, it won't be a secret any more!' "

In Lois Gould's fantasy world X won't have sex-linked behavior forced upon it until it nears maturity and its primary and secondary sex characteristics matter. She challenges us to raise X's and the baby Y, who appears at the end of the story, as well as W's and Z's of our own. Gould's message is clear: we should stop thinking of children as girls and boys.

"Think of children as people. Too many think of them as boys and girls," says Mark Lundeen of the Bank Street College of Education in New York City. "They are not thinking of childhood as a developmental stage of people. As long as people are using that terminology, like 'boy and girl,' as long as they are using the flag words, we won't move ahead. If people are talking to you about 'the negroes today' you know where they are at. Anybody who is saying 'boys or girls' is at the same place. There are seldom instances where you should use that. We say, 'There are three children on their sleds.' Most of them are boys, but now our daughter does not feel excluded. She is a child. So are they."

Studies cited in Eleanor Emmons Maccoby and Carol Nagy Jacklin's *The Psychology of Sex Differences* illustrate the different ways boys and girls are treated. Though they find no conclusive proof that children *consistently* are treated differently because of their sexes, they do find that children are reinforced for engaging in sex-typed behavior. So boys will be boys and girls will be girls. Or boys will be as they are told boys should be, and the same goes for girls.

Children realize very early that there are two sexes. Some professionals think a child knows her sexual identity by the age of six months; others say eighteen months is the age of identification. In addition to learning there are two sexes, children learn that one is more highly valued than the other. Blue is better than pink. The king in a deck of cards is higher than the queen. "He" comes before "she" in a sentence. The sexist lesson is everywhere. Male is considered better than female.

In *The Liberated Man*, Warren Farrell asserts that children of kindergarten age prefer the activities of the male parent. The man who goes out into the world is viewed as more exciting. "My three-year-old says she wants to be a man when she grows up," says one big-city reporter home on her second maternity leave. "She doesn't remember when I went out to work every day. Now Jim is seen as fun. I'm the drudge."

Almost every nursery-school staff can tick off the names and stories of little girls who wanted to be, or insisted they were, boys. Much scarcer are the tales of boys who wanted to be girls. Both girls and boys who see their mothers without power, money, or respect want to avoid growing up and assuming the same position.

Sigmund Freud labeled penis envy as one of the afflictions women suffer. Some in the psychological professions still believe penis envy is organ envy. They don't understand that there's a great difference between "Gee, what is that?" and "I want one — I'm incomplete without one."

"The woman suffering this terrible trauma, realizing she doesn't have what a man has, is not what the people of my school, the interpersonal school of psychological thinking, believe," offers Dr. Robert E. Gould. "This all symbolizes what is better about being a man than a woman in this world, wholly symbolized by the penis, man's much more powerful role in this world, more advantageous role. If women had all the advantages the men had and the men were as disadvantaged as the women, then we would find men would have vagina envy and breast envy — symbolic of what makes the woman different. After all, the breast is much more obvious to a child than a penis. The child is on the breast, sees the breast — there are two of them, and often they are probably less covered than a penis. One would think there would be breast envy — the child even has the experience of knowing what the breast can do, and doesn't know what a penis can do. I really think this makes for the differences between the sexes. All little girls say they want to be little boys. Why? Because they know that little boys have it so much better in this world. Penis envy was a very true thing about the power of men. As a biological theory it is not valid."

Penis envy. Penis pride. There is tremendous reverence for children with penises — they hold the power. More than one preschool teacher had stories affirming that little girls know boys are more powerful. "In our school the girls ask the boys, 'Will you marry me?' " said one preschool teacher. "The boys get to say, 'Yes' or 'No.' They have the power, the girls think so."

Many feminist families have tried to explain to their boy children what it is like to be female, to be without power, in our culture. Some parents are more successful than others in making the secondary position of females real to the sons. One New England parent who has tried to develop her son's sensitivity to the oppression of women and minorities is nonetheless pessimistic about the possibilities of undoing the message of the culture. "My son has lived through the slogans. We have a poster of Joan of Arc over the supper table that reads, 'I have to go home now and fix supper.' The issue of sharing housework is part of our lives. Randy does half the housework, sews his own buttons. I have worked for ten years, but somehow the idea that men are superior to women, or that men enjoy options denied women, is so societally ingrained that I think at best you can get a sexist child who feels guilty about it. He'll catch himself every once in a while. We have to strive for it.

"I think it is near impossible to raise non-racist children. My husband works with poor black families in his family-care medical practice. A good portion of our close friends are black, but still my kids feel kindly and compassionate toward black kids. They have heard the stories about how hard it is for black people, but I suspect they feel different and still slightly superior. At least they are attributing that to circumstance, not heredity, but they think black kids are poor kids."

Although feminist families often experience the fight against sexism as three-steps-forward-and-two-steps-back, there is at least that one step ahead. What is in it for our children if we are able to break through the sex-role stereotypes and raise them as free, fair-minded human beings? The assets are seen in high relief when contrasted with what has been the norm.

What will non-sexist childraising do for girls?

1. You can be a success. You don't have to marry a successful man, or marry to be successful yourself.

2. You can dream your dreams and live them, too.

3. You can celebrate your strength.

4. You can celebrate and parade your intelligence.

5. You won't be judged by your looks alone.

6. You can know that aggressive and feminine traits can coexist in the same woman.

7. You will know your own life will not stop with the birth of your children. You will share the parenting, housework and child care with the children's father.

8. You won't be pitied if you mother only girls. You won't bask in praise if you mother a son.

9. You won't worry that you're a bad mother if you leave your children to go to work.

10. You can admit your sexuality.

11. You can like or loathe things without questioning your womanliness:

a. ballet and music
b. spectator sports
c. contact sports
d. guns
e. cars
f. clothes
g. miniatures
h. flowers
i. carpentry and tools
j. add whatever made you doubt yourself

12. You will suffer less alcoholism and mental depression.

13. You can rest easy making more money than a man, even if that man is your husband.

What will non-sexist childraising do for boys?

1. You will know you aren't destined to be the sole support of your wife and kids. You will have a partner in your wife.

2. You will know you don't have to be a hulking football player before you're allowed to do needlepoint.

3. You can cry unashamedly when you are hurt. You can sport a flaccid upper lip.

4. You can compete and admit when you've lost.

5. You can admit fear. Your emotions needn't be kept under wraps.

6. You can acknowledge affection for a man, even hug and kiss him.

7. You can be close friends with a woman. You need not consider her a sex object or "a piece of ass."

8. You will be independent and competent in life's skills — cooking, cleaning, sewing, laundry, child care.

9. You can like or loathe things without questioning your manliness:

a. ballet and music
b. spectator sports
c. contact sports
d. guns
e. cars
f. clothes

g. miniatures
h. flowers
i. carpentry and tools
j. add whatever made you doubt yourself

10. You won't be considered a lesser man if you father only girls. You won't be considered a "real stud" if you produce boys.

11. You will suffer fewer heart attacks and ulcers.

12. You won't measure your worth by the size of your paycheck — or your penis.

Some children are already reaping the harvest of non-sexist upbringing. Their young consciousnesses are raised. They see their own horizons as defined by personality and choice, not by sex.

"Our six-year-old daughter has a sense of herself as a pioneer child. She knows she is a different breed of girl," reports a parent proudly. "She told us this wonderful story about being with Chip and some other kids who said, 'Girls can't throw a ball as far as boys can.' 'Oh, yes, girls can!' she announced. Now, she told us this story very dramatically —

how she stepped up, took the ball, and threw it farther than any of them! She has a great feeling of excitement."

"My kid is a five-year-old feminist," says one mother in publishing. "The only T-shirts she wants to wear either have a picture of Wonder Woman or are printed with feminist slogans. At five she's a militant feminist."

"My eight-year-old daughter brought home a workbook from school last year with some sexist examples that she picked up very quickly and pointed out to me," said one psychiatrist mother. "The workbook asked, Which toys do girls like to play with? There was a kite and a ball and a doll. 'Well, how am I supposed to answer this one?' she asked me. 'I know what they mean, but that's not fair.' She had thought through what they expected of her and refused to buckle under."

"At five, Sarah is no longer an innocent feminist, no longer naïve," says a mother. "She's had some experiences with sex prejudice. Now she is savvy. We talk about 'they' and 'we.' Sarah has applied it to her life. When she sees something on TV, or someone says something that is degrading to women, Sarah will comment, 'Mama, they think girls are afraid, but we know better, don't we?' We certainly do."

One mother who came to feminism ten years ago, long after her son who is now a college student was out of diapers, thinks he may well be less sexist than his classmates even though his formative years were over before her feminism was formed. She considers her role in his consciousness raising important, but feels his continuing education is in the hands of his peers. "His contemporaries, his women friends raise his consciousness and direct his behavior. Since he is a junior now, I guess he should be thinking about making a living. I am encouraging him to take the course that will broaden him as a person. While with my daughters, I find myself saying, 'Think about business. Try those hard courses. Don't avoid economics because you think you may not do well.' I guess I'm doing the reverse of the traditional. But I assume my son will earn a living, so I'm encouraging the part of him society may ignore, and the same for my daughters."

Many teachers are in a quandary about how to interest students in sexism on a deeper level. "The sophomores I teach are jaded about sexism," compains one high-school teacher. "They've had it all. They've heard the anti-sexist line in elementary school and in junior high, but they know this society wants gentle, quiet women and tough men. So far, I've been unable to interest them on a more substantial level. I think the kids are very aware on a superficial level of the whole popularity of sexism. They can talk about it. The kids see very clearly and very differently the roles of mother and father. They see that mother takes care of us. The mother may work, but she also cooks all the meals and makes sure we are on schedule.

"Even the high-school kids who are highly politicized and very sensitive sound sexist some of the time. They are only human and the language, for example, has only been liberated the last couple of years. The other day a boy got up in town meeting to argue a point he felt strongly about. He said, 'Will the chairman . . .' and another kid piped up, correcting him, 'chairPERSON.' The boy nodded, acknowledged his mistake, and began again. 'Will the chairman . . .' again the correction, 'chairPERSON.' The boy knew what was fair, wanted to use the right terminology, but the word 'chairman' was so ingrained that he couldn't remember to use the politically correct word in the heat of the moment. He was too busy worrying about the substance of his argument."

The liberation of children is under way. Not all children have been touched by liberation, and not all who have been touched have been liberated. But more and more children and adolescents are learning that cooking, sewing, and cleaning are tasks *people*, not just women, do. They are being taught respect for both sexes. They are being told their options are open, and some are believing what they've been told.

"I'm really impressed with the way these kids talk, very matter of fact," says one Long Island guidance counselor. "The girls think nothing of planning to be veterinarians or lawyers. They are thinking of careers — plural. They are flexible and can see themselves in one profession or another. When I was a little girl I thought I'd be a secretary or a teacher, like my mother. One of my friends aspired to be a diplomat's wife. This year I have all seniors. The women are a very different breed."

Yes, the women growing up today are a very different breed. Besides taking control of their own careers, they are also learning to take control of their own bodies. "We're raising some very macho little girls these days," commented one father. "I see my son's friends. Some of those girls are tough — I wouldn't want to mess with them. I'm surprised he gets along so well. Can we raise children who are strong without their being tough? I don't know." Another parent, a mother, defends teaching her daughter to be tough: "I'd rather have her tough — and even obnoxious — than passive. I don't want her pushed around. She's going to get a lot of humility lessons, just being a woman. I'm not going to give her one."

Sports has been one arena where the players with the best control over their bodies, singularly or as a team, had a good chance of controlling the game, and winning. They won pennants and trophies and conference titles for downing opponents. They acquired pride in their bodies and developed strength just by competing. The stereotypic picture has actually been true to life. The boys played and the girls cheered them on. Boys trained their bodies for a season of their chosen sport. Out of that some got sports scholarships to college. The fellows who got through the season ended up with developed muscles and physical endurance. All the girls developed were large thigh muscles from practicing the cheerleader's jump, or hip bruises from marching with a megaphone clasped too tightly to their sides. Boys got in shape. Girls were a shape.

Sadly, too many girls who were rejected as pompom shakers felt worthless. So did the guys who never made the squad. Nobody cared if the washout who had been number 14 was in shape or not. When they judged him inadequate, they threw him off the bench. Dr. Melvin Levine, a pediatrician at Children's Hospital in Boston, reports that he sees boys of eight and nine who can't catch a ball. They feel like third-class citizens. They're afraid to go down to the bus stop. The chances of a little boy taking dancing or collecting butterflies are pretty slim. He's only supposed to be a tough hockey end. These troubled boys come in with headaches, bellyaches, wounded self-esteem.

"We have sports that the bad athlete can play. We encourage them to play the great equalizers, those sports nobody does well. In America, the schleppy kid can play soccer as well as the good one. These kids even like crab soccer, where the kids get down on their backs and walk like crabs. They kick this huge medicine ball. The non-athletes love it. We try to get these bad athletes not to play sports. I am the state champion gym-excuse writer. I'm an ally. We greatly exaggerate body consciousness in this country."

Many parents and teachers are actively de-emphasizing "making the team" or winning the division championship. "To paraphrase, it matters not how he plays the game. I don't care if he does play the game," admitted a parent. "I don't like sports and I am not embarrassed to tell him that. I don't have to throw a ball around with him to be a good father. I'm liberated enough to know that. But is he? I don't know. Peer pressure is tremendous," said a non-athletic father.

"I don't like sports" and "We frown on competitive team sports" was an often-repeated theme. It applied to boys as well as girls. "Being on something like a tennis team is the best," offered another parent. "There's an individual challenge and a team spirit, without the head bashing craziness you see in other sports."

While the pressure to excel in sports is easing on boys, it is increasing on girls. "Will girls be humiliated if they don't earn their letter? I hope not!" said one mother. "I love to see girls play in teams," said another, the mother of two boys. "I watched two women's teams playing softball today and things are different. They play. They are serious. If the third-base player missed the ball and the other team got a triple on what should have been a single, nobody laughed. Nobody looked over at her boyfriend and giggled. They were there to play, not show off."

One father of a boy and a girl likes having both his kids in Little League. Showing off a picture of both kids suited up for a game, he confided, "I can dine out on this picture in liberal feminist circles. Caroline started in Little League in California, where if you can walk, you can play. She turned out to be a good hitter, after she spent time in the field and learned some skills. Here in New York, at least on the West Side of Manhattan, an unskilled boy or girl has a problem. You have no place to learn the skills. You can play only if you have the experience. How do you get the experience? Of the four West Side Little League teams, only four players are girls."

The women who have grown up athletic in America, even those who have made the Olympic team, admit it has been difficult to reconcile femininity and athletic bodies. A group of young female Olympic athletes discussed their experiences on a television talk show. Women are taught, they said, and encouraged not to be strong so they will conform to the classic idea of what a beautiful woman is. Muscles are not considered beautiful on a female body. "Look at my legs," offered a non-Olympic dancer. "These muscles are just too developed to be sexually attractive. They don't make it when compared with the ideal."

If the ideal woman isn't allowed to have muscles, we must change the ideal. Athena doesn't look like a shrinking violet in marble. What about her? Wonder Woman lifts cars and displays superhuman strength. Wonder Woman, however, couldn't be a candidate for a strong-looking ideal woman. Take a look at her — there's not a developed muscle in sight.

Men are supposed to be strong; women are supposed to be weak. Men are supposed to be aggressive; women are supposed to be passive. The fact that our society demands different behavior and different achievement from boys and from girls sometimes has dire consequences.

One parent explained how sexist attitudes interfered with her son's development: "They said he was rowdy and slow 'because he's a boy.' It turns out he doesn't see things straight. He has a learning disability. They wanted to ignore the symptoms because he is a boy." Dr. Melvin Levine asserts, "Here and all over the world there is a seven to one ratio, boys to girls, in who has problems." Admissions to mental hospitals for patients of pediatric age are six or seven to one, boys. "That," offers Dr. Levine, "may well be a secondary reaction to cultural conditioning that does not allow boys to express fear. Because we are culturally less demanding of girls to achieve and more demanding of boys, the boys get referred to us younger. The strategy of failures is different for boys and for girls. Girls adopt a very quiet, passive, inconspicuous, compulsive, very neat posture. They fade into the wall. The same problems in boys will show up by their raising hell, smashing everything in sight. What we find is that because of the styles they adopt, the average age of the girls referred to us is much older than the boys. Teachers and parents are more likely to refer a boy who is destroying everything, and not worry about a quiet girl. What happens is the girl has a worse chance to recover."

Severely troubled youngsters, as well as officially untroubled ones, would benefit if "boys played house more often, and girls played war," says Dr. Levine. Boys have been taught to deny their own softness, or at best to hide it in shame. "In this day and age it is still a shock for me to see a boy cry in school," observes one elementary school teacher. "It is embarrassing for the class and the child. Girls can cry. It's expected."

Even the parents who preach "you can cry if you want to" to their sons often have trouble dealing with the tears. "Russell, who is eight, tells me it is okay to cry and he fights for that right. Considering my upbringing, crying is hard for me," says a divorced mother. "My family told me, 'Come on, you can handle it.' Crying to me was weak."

"*Children* cry. Anybody who says a boy shouldn't cry is a sexist pig. Anybody who 'has trouble' with a little boy's tears should have her head examined," said an irate mother.

"We talk about crying in a course I teach," said a high-school teacher. "The kids say it is wrong. They see their mothers cry, but hardly ever their fathers. Boys share a whole lot about crying as kids and being spanked if they kept crying."

"It's All Right to Cry" daily blares forth from many "Free to Be You and Me" phonograph albums. The children are listening; so, apparently, are the politicians. What a far cry 1976 was from 1972 — literally! In 1972, Edmund Muskie's presidential campaign hit the skids after the country watched him cry in the snows of New Hampshire. He read a dirty-trick letter conceived by the Nixon pranksters, and it reduced him to tears. Four short years later presidential nominees of both parties cried on television. Gerald Ford teared up on returning to his home turf in Michigan. Jimmy Carter cried to his friends in Plains, Georgia, thanking them for the help that elected him. In two election years, four years apart, three national politicians — men — spilled over with tears. In 1972, Edmund Muskie was done in by crying. In 1976 two crying men survived. Clearly, the times are changing. Centuries-old patterns of childraising are being eroded and broken down. The sex-role track children are set in at birth is being buried. Some parents and professionals, however, caution about rocking the sexist boat. They ask, "Is it healthy to do so?,"

"Just because we don't know exactly what the differences are between male and female doesn't mean they don't exist," warned a senior faculty member of a school of education. Another educator cautioned that until we know the consequences of changing the way we bring up boys and girls, we shouldn't alter anything. That, however, becomes a chicken-or-egg-first question. If we are going to move, we are told to do it slowly — to take it easy lest we upset the mystical balance of the sexes and somehow undermine all of Western civilization.

Western civilization could do with some shaking up. Would the Western world, or the Eastern world for that matter, be in the state it is if women had had a bigger part to play? The world of our children has a better chance of surviving and flourishing if both sexes share the direction.

9

HOMOPHOBIA

PARENTS don't want their sons to become homosexuals, and they don't want their daughters to marry homosexuals. The opposite possibilities aren't considered nearly so often. Many parents are afraid that a program of non-sexist child-raising will turn their sons gay, that sex roles will be confused and sexual preference perverted. Female homosexuality is neither scorned nor feared to the degree male homosexuality is

This is not to say lesbians are treated fairly or equally. They are discriminated against in employment. They lose custody of their children, as Mary Jo Risher did in Texas last year. But men are not threatened by gay women, so the male world isn't either. It has been argued that men don't feel threatened by penis-less love making. In fact, many are excited by it, as demonstrated by the multiple four-color-process layouts in the slick men's skin magazines like *Playboy* and *Penthouse* of women making love to women. The straight men who are the readership of those magazines are titillated by homosexuality, as long as it is female homosexuality.

What causes lesbianism? The reasons are really unknown. Unlike male homosexuality, lesbianism hasn't been studied very much. Those who have studied the causes of lesbianism have not looked beyond the family as the causative agent. In his book *Lesbianism*, David Rosen cites a 1971 study in which H. E. Kaye examined 157 lesbians and found "the close-binding, intimate father" to be the counterpart to the "close-binding mother" found in the studies of male homosexuality.

Rosen also cites a 1965 study by E. Bene that concludes that lesbians were more "hostile towards and afraid of their fathers than were the married women, and they felt more often that their fathers were weak and incompetent."

Both Bene and Dr. David Rosen offered the opinion that the parents' wish for a son correlates with the homosexuality of their daughter. Does Rosen's 1974 study of 26 lesbians, all Daughters of Bilitis (a militant lesbian organization) tell us more about lesbianism and its causes, or just flesh out 26 case studies? Rosen admits that he found no universal causal pattern. However, in 23 of 26 cases the women grew up in an unstable family.

In our male-oriented culture female sexual preference matters less than male preference. To parents, it doesn't seem to be of real concern. Pediatrician Melvin Levine says, "I can never remember a parent coming to me in all these years — twelve of them — worried that their daughter is a homosexual. Parents will walk into a bedroom, find two girls having a sleep-over party with their clothes off, lying next to one another, comparing one to the other, and the parents will laugh about it. Two boys in bed together doing the same thing (which is perfectly normal behavior in young girls and boys) — the whole world falls in. I get calls late at night. I tell parents to cool it. They had no right walking into that room. They should play it down."

Levine says, "I don't think there is any greater fear that parents in this country have than that their son may be a homosexual. I think if I told some parents that their son was going blind, or had a terrible disease, they might find these things more acceptable than if I told them he was a homosexual. The guilt is terrific. Also the way it reflects on them. If a kid is going blind, it's not because of anything they did. If anything, they get benefits, like 'Look at these wonderful people coping with a blind son.' You are not going to hear anyone say, 'Look at these wonderful people dealing with their homosexual nineteen-year-old."

If the onus was lifted from the family as the cause of homosexuality, the guilt would also be lifted and with it some of the parental pain.

Right now, parents are blamed for a son's homosexuality and to some extent congratulated when daughters act like boys. "Somehow we are amused by a tomboy," offers a pediatrician, "but we are frightened and never call a boy 'effeminate.'"

Many homosexuals act more female than male. In this culture that is despised. Being a woman is scorned, but a man who abdicates what society dictates is his manliness, and chooses to behave more like a woman, is loathed.

What causes a man to become a homosexual? Professionals don't feel that encouraging a boy to take ballet, for example, will put him on the road to homosexuality, but they do caution that the derision a pioneering boy could be subject to might damage him profoundly.

"One of our sons is taking dance for his gym class," said one psychiatrist. "In school he is the only boy among ten girls taking it. We have no feeling that this will turn him into a homosexual. We think this will be useful for him in a lot of ways — as long as he feels comfortable and not 'out of it' doing it. But if he feels he couldn't take the teasing that he might get, then we would have to sadly and reluctantly feel that he should give up something worthwhile because the public pressure would be too much. So that kind of thing goes on all the time. Some you win and some you lose."

If it is a boy's choice to break the mold, that is one thing, but if it is foisted upon him, that is something else. Offers one doctor, "A mother says, 'I'd like my little boy to be less of a sexist' and goes out and buys him leotards. He's the only boy in the ballet class. The boys in his class see a picture in the paper of him in leotards and drive him crazy. I couldn't recommend that for a child. They'd be calling him a fag.

"I don't think I would ask a family to suggest their 12-year-old son walk to school holding hands with the neighbor's 12-year-old son, or ask the kid to wear a dress. I would worry about him and what he would have to endure. I would wonder if the kid would have the stamina to endure what he would face. Changes have to take place on a societal, not just familial, level. Remember, we didn't go to a particular black family and say, 'Sit in the front of the bus.'"

Another professional asserts that it is a child's culture that either rewards or ridicules him. Carol Nadelson, psychiatrist and parent, says she is fighting sexism professionally and personally. "My son loves to cook, and is very good at it. He does it in an environment where everyone says, 'Isn't that terrific!' His father cooks. He needs to feel that is an okay thing for a boy to do. He likes to cook more than he likes to play ball at times. He needs to be told it is all right not to be athletic."

The women's movement is a political movement, one that seeks to change the foundations of the patriarchical culture in which we live. The parents who are actively working to change their own lives and their children's lives know that the women's movement is one of shifting and sharing power. It is not a sexual movement. Nevertheless, parents and professionals alike fear that if you encourage a boy to be gentle, give him a doll, teach him how to navigate his way around the kitchen, and teach him the value of girls and women, you will turn him into a homosexual.

One reason for the fear is the cruelty of the little-boy culture. Boys who are different suffer.

"The pressures on school-age boys are enormous," one pediatricial reported. "And they are exerted by other school-age boys. There are three diagnoses a nine-year-old can have. He can be considered 'cool' — a cool guy — which is the best thing. He can be considered 'mental' — which means he does crazy things, like goes to see the reading specialist, or goes to a special school. As in, 'The mental bus picks him up every morning.' Mental is a very big thing among nine-year-olds."

It is also real bad to be the third thing, a fag. "Boys this age don't have any idea what homosexuality is. So 'fag' has no homosexual connotations. It means an ineffective male. It has something to do with being a little more like a girl than a boy. It is subtle. When you are a boy, there is nothing worse than being a girl."

"A fag is a kid who doesn't want to wear a uniform in school every day. He doesn't have the right kind of blue jeans. He's wearing laced shoes, everybody else is in sneakers. Or, he combs his hair the wrong way, or he talks to girls. Anyone who violates the code is called a fag."

Why is it that if a boy doesn't conform to the John Wayne stereotype of what it is to be male, the only other species he can be is homosexual? Any deviation from the image of tough-guy-shoot-em-up is considered proof positive that the kid is queer. Any deviation — flower smelling, piano playing, cooking, anything that girls like to do — can be ample reason to label a boy as inferior and suspect.

If it is feminine, it is less valuable. It is also suspect and threatening sexually. Remember the scorn heaped upon Elvis Presley? The adults were scared to death of him in the mid-fifties because he was sexy, not because of his puffy hair, or his sweet voice. It was his hips, and the way he moved them, that drove parents wild. He moved his hips more like the way girls in the tight, straight skirts of the fifties moved their hips than the way any self-respecting male greaser would move. He moved his hips like a girl, they said. He was disgusting.

What about the Beatles? With long hair like females they *had* to be queer. They adopted traditionally female hair styles and were scorned for it, and labeled not really men. But then there occurred a mass re-education about the history of hair styles and what length hair men can wear and still be men. George Washington wore a pony tail. Long-haired eighteenth-century French courtiers were cocksmen! The hirsute threat to male sexual preference was exploded.

The hair argument was used in the same way against radicals, hippies, and even moderates, in the late 1960s. Their politics were opposed, their sexual preference questioned, and their value, in the eyes of the world, diminished because they grew their hair long, like women, and wore bright colors and jewelry.

What is this male homosexuality and why is everyone so frightened of catching it? Parents so fear that their sons will turn gay that even a small boy's desire to try on a dress can greatly disturb them. One therapist is already worried about what she will answer if her four-month-old son is old enough to ask if he can wear a dress. "How could I let him wear a dress to the playground? He'd be teased unmercifully. What shall I say, 'Yes,' then wheel him out to the lions? Maybe he just won't ask. He will know he's a boy by then. He'll notice his father doesn't wear a dress. Politically I am torn. I don't want to say, 'Boys don't do that.' Before he was born, I thought, if I have a son who asks to wear nail polish I won't let him. It wouldn't be healthy. Now, I know I'll say, 'Okay.' The nail polish is no big deal, but the dress upsets me."

One mother of two sons, who is a carpenter and a playwright, bought wardrobes for her boys in varying colors and textures once she noticed how drab their clothing was. She picked up an array of nubby corduroy, soft cotton, plush velour, as well as flannel, nylon, and wool. The colors were the spectrum. The boys enjoyed coordinating their own colors and wearing rough and smooth together. They played with some of her dresses and scarves.

"I had such a shock the first time I saw him dressed up in a long dress and a scarf. I'm sure I didn't handle it right. It was just that I felt that it wasn't what he should be doing. I mean, he just looked too *pretty*. At first I thought, well, maybe he's going through some kind of identity crisis and I should reinforce the fact that he's a boy — maybe he doesn't know it yet. I would say things like, 'Ethan, you're a great boy,' and I would underline the word *boy*. One day he just looked at me and said, 'Of course I'm a boy,' and gave me this withering look." The child was not confused about his sex, but his mother was worried that allowing her son to dress up, coupled with her feminist politics, would transform Ethan into a homosexual.

The fear that a preschool boy will become homosexual often is voiced most loudly after a parent visits nursery school, or day-care center, and sees the boy in what the parent considers inappropriate clothing from the dress-up corner of the classroom.

"We battle a lot of parents," one preschool assistant director said. "We battled Jody's father when he arrived at the classroom to find Jody in a pink tutu and his own big curls. That father almost went through the roof. The mother understood Jody's need to just try on different clothes, but she warned us never to let his father see him in that costume again."

Another preschool teacher explained the need she sees in

children who dress up. "I've seen the long transition of children who dress up over my years in preschool. What the children do is dress up like mother, to recreate the mother role, the closeness. They wear things women wear to role play, to bring mother and the experience of mother closer. To be something for a while they cannot be — a woman for a while, a man for a while — is important for kids under five.

Even at Little Red Schoolhouse in Greenwich Village, where liberalism and progressivism have a long history and where the student body is parented by hip, sophisticated New Yorkers, parents fear homosexuality. "I overheard two fathers, cool, hip, watching their sons in the dress-up corner say, 'I guess our sons will grow up to be pansies.' Their fear was real. That was the unstated, unconscious, emotional gut response," said one parent.

In a New Jersey day-care center a father came upon his son in women's clothes. After he ordered, "Get that off," the father listened and at least gave lip service to the idea. "The boy is very gentle inside with a macho overlay. His gentle side was not being spoken to at all. He was physically violent, hyperactive. Dressing up like that allowed him to feel closer to his mother."

Early childhood educators know that dressing up doesn't cause homosexuality or transvestism. Parents, however, don't understand this. "I don't identify fantasy play with gender development," one male preschool professional offered. "But the boys are just not as loose about dressing up as girls are. I've noticed the transition from a pre-media conditioning. It is especially true from the twos to the threes. In the two-year-old room, there will be Sammy in the dress-up corner, but will he be there next year? I don't know."

Some parents fear that even limited exposure to female clothes will alter their son's sexual preference. Even barrettes have the potential for doing it. In one upper-middle-class preschool in Springfield, Massachusetts, the director found a set of parents agitated that their two-year-old son loved putting his sister's barrettes in his hair. No amount of reassurance from the director allowed the parents to relax about those barrettes. "His hair's been cut — nowhere to put the barrettes any more."

"There is nothing you have to deny a girl," the mother of a son commented. "But with Jake that is different. I don't want to tell him straight out what boys don't do, but my gut says to me, 'Oops, boys don't do that.' I experience an uneasy fear that if I experiment with him, he'll be damaged sexually. It is my job to guide him. It would be easier to guide a girl."

One secure mother of an eight-year-old son was aghast to hear what a mother had to say. "She said that at twelve, her son was a flaming heterosexual and he wanted *Penthouse* magazine. I told her I was more interested in nurturing the gentle side of a boy than worrying about other things in the world. I'm less worried about him becoming a homosexual than him being a person who treated women and people in a negative way or was physically brutal."

One teacher and mother of three is concerned that homosexuality is out of the closet. She was disturbed by a Mary Quant makeup-for-men advertisement that ran in national magazines in the spring of last year. The picture shows a middle-aged man in business suit looking down into a compact and applying silvery lavender eye shadow. The teacher described him as, "This older man, who to me looks like an old queen, getting his makeup on. Just how equal do you want to make these things?

"There may be a liberal person who says, this is perfectly all right. But I'll tell you pointblank, I am not liberal. My son is nine. And my girls aren't grown. Until they get quite far along, I have no intention of giving them too much leeway on sexual preference. I intend to push — certainly brainwash. I think being a man means being tender and strong. I will still teach my children that to be a homosexual is an abnormal thing. Sorry, that's my viewpoint. Personally, I stick toward the middle. There are many situations whereby it is intimated that it is kinky, not abnormal, that it's all right once in a while. Does makeup make a man gay? The particular man in that ad looks gay. If we were living in an Indian society and we painted ourselves, then that would be fine. Until it is firmly established, no."

The fear of homosexuality is pervasive, but dissatisfaction with the kind of heterosexual world we live in also exists in pockets of this country.

"What's so terrific about this so-called heterosexual world we live in?" asks Dr. Selma Greenberg. "We live in a homosexual world now. There's a separate world for each sex. Most women spend time with women in those ghettoes we call suburbs. Most men spend time with men. Once a week, missionary position, is not heterosexuality. Do we want *this* heterosexual life?"

Commuter trains full of men traveling to and from the female segregated suburbs, executive suites of men flanked by typing pools of women — do we want to promote a world of all men in insurance and all women in elementary education? That world is the so-called heterosexual world. Do you want it? We do not dare call it a homosexual world where men lunch together, sweat together on the construction site, sweat together on the ball field, or swear together at the card table. But where are the women? Where *is* the heterosexuality if the sexes don't mix?

When we are, at some point in the future, free of the unnamed and limitless demands and expectations of what it is to be a man or a woman, then we will be free to be just people — we will be free to mingle and be truly heterosexual. The shes may doubt they are "really women" and the hes may doubt they are "really men," but none of the skeptical self-doubting women and men doubt that they are really people. It is the sex label that clouds our perceptions and alters our expectations.

If the sex label is removed does that mean we will all approach sameness? Not according to Dr. Robert E. Gould. "I don't think all men and women are going to be alike. There will be just as many differences between men and women, and in some places the women will be playing the role traditionally thought of as male, and the man will be playing the role thought of as female."

Gould does project a change in sexual behavior once personalities are freed from sex-stereotyping. He sees "an increase in bisexuality in the future. I think everybody is basically bisexual and they limit it when they feel that homosexuality is frowned upon, at the very least, and condemned, at the most. Most people would be bisexual, and that would be something healthy. Personal experiences and taste, as well as genetic and biological factors, would determine how people behave. One person would be more heterosexual, one more homosexual — each one maintaining some sort of bisexual interest. Very few would be fifty-fifty. A person of one sex would choose a person of another sex on the basis of person and personality, not sex. It would be all mixed together, but not creating a situation detrimental to the world in general. I think opposites still attract each other in many ways and would complement each other."

Homosexuality is not about to return to the closet. Bisexuality is on the rise. Professional psychiatric associations have removed the pathological label from homosexuality. Although it is argued that the re-labeling resulted from political pressure from gay activist groups, it does bespeak a liberalizing among mental health professionals.

Despite our society's rampant homophobia and anti-homosexual prejudice, however, psychiatrists and psychologists note the irony that parents fear heterosexuality more than homosexuality. Parents actively encourage deep relationships with children of the same sex, while at the same time they "tell little boys to stay away from little girls and they tell girls not to let a boy come near them," writes Dr. June Singer in her book *Androgny*.

Promoting fear of the opposite sex in childhood may make it hard to emerge from the normal homosexual period in early adolescence into a life of adult heterosexuality. Dr. Singer urges parents to prompt girls and boys to "learn the value of each sex" and to help children "see the importance of being able to relate to *both* sexes in terms of friendship and affection." In other words, to practice non-sexist childraising.

10

DEPROGRAMMING THE CULTURE —
TOGS, TELEVISION, AND TOYS

PARENTS living the stereotype, or living a proto-type, all share the same problems in deprogramming the sexist culture we live in. The culture, the media, tell boys and girls what toys to play with, what clothes to wear, what length to wear their hair. What can feminist parents do about the very strong message that comes from print, television, and movies?

One approach some parents take in deprogramming the culture is to dress their offspring like children, not like girls and boys. Traditional boys' clothes — even their dress-up clothes — are more functional than girls' clothing. Long pants are warmer than dresses; they protect bare legs from scrapes and pain. Dress sashes come untied, catch on things, and generally look untidy when they are loose. Boys' clothes are dyed dark colors so the dirt won't show. Girls' clothes are pastel. They turn up tell-tale dirt if girls try to play like boys. Boys' shoes are made sturdy — to run in. Girls' shoes are made slight and slippery — to walk in.

Parents who dress their children so they can be active and comfortable sometimes find their girl children mistaken for boys. "We've taken a position on clothing and hair — nothing that is non-functional. Mostly the girls are dressed in overalls, or slacks and a shirt. The whole family has short hair, because it seems more practical.

"Some people will say, 'Hello, little boy.' Our older daughter answers, 'You think I am a boy because I have short hair.' When she was young all we had to do was put her in some sex-stereotyped clothes, and before we got to the lobby, somebody who knows her would make some stereotypic remark like, 'You look very cute, little girl.' They would immediately refer to her as a girl. We stopped putting her in 'girlish' clothes because no matter what we did with her, she would get all sorts of stereotyped feedback from those around her. Now she dresses like a kid. The same person will see her and say, 'Hi, how are you today?' " said one set of parents.

Parents who strive for unisex baby clothing sometimes have a difficult task. One mother rejected all sex-stereotyped baby clothes. She even steered clear of lambs and ducks and the entire fuzzy animal school of decorating children's clothes. She wanted her child to reflect their way of life. They ate organic foods. They wore bright-colored sensible clothing. Her favorite baby clothes were tie-dyed, so she tie-dyed the pastels. Unfortunately she made a mistake. When the baby peed, he ended up tie-dyed. The colors were not set.

Another mother reported that when her daughter was born, pink baby clothes arrived from the local department stores and from relatives in another state. Her first impulse was to exchange the stereotyped pink-is-for-a-girl clothes for a different color, or stack the gift boxes in the closet. But, it was hard for her to run from store to store with clothing to exchange when she had a few weeks' old infant making demands. Also, it was a shame to waste perfectly good stretch suits and shirts and overalls. Keeping her daughter out of pink was important, though. Pink showed the dirt easily. Pink meant soft, something she did not want her daughter to be. Pink meant weak not strong, passive not active, pastel not vibrant. Pink had too many stereotypic connotations.

The young mother decided to dye the clothes black. One vat of black dye transformed the clothes from unacceptable to acceptable, and from innocent to sophisticated and sexy and evil. The movie *Rosemary's Baby* had been released two years before. It ended with Satan's infant son dressed in black and lying in a black satin bassinet. Maybe it was the devil in Sarah's mother that wanted to shock passersby who'd be chucking little Sarah under the chin. She says she dyed the clothes black to be sensible. It is a good color for crawling babies; it doesn't show the dirt.

"We could have dressed Nicholas to look like a typical eighteen-month-old boy," said another mother. "We could have put him in a little blue suit, cut his long curls. We could have done that, but we didn't want to. It did disturb my husband, more than it did me, when people mistook him for a girl. And I have to admit, I didn't put him in pink. I don't like it much anyway."

Parents of girls, by and large, feel a greater need to control their children's wardrobes. All boys clothing is acceptable to most parents, while lots of female clothing is deemed inappropriate. Some parents feel their sons can learn sexism from their clothing, however, and they censor their sons' wardrobes, too.

These parents discourage their sons from wearing clothes with what they call a "macho theme." Shirts with "I'm a li'l slugger" and printed with a picture of a baseball player are never part of their wardrobes. Nor are numbered sports jerseys, nor shirts with flaming racing cars careening across the chest. They do not want to encourage their sons to take part in competitive team sports. They do want to discourage the violence of football and racing. He'll get enough of that encouragement from the culture, they say. He doesn't need it at home or on his chest.

Many little girls go through a stage when wearing dresses is terribly important. On the coldest days they will reject pants in favor of thin tights and a billowy skirt. At about age four, these girls will wear floor-length party dresses and party shoes every day, effectively immobilizing themselves in the playground and in the block corner, and making them prissy at the easel. They want to wear dresses even though their mothers may not have had skirts on in weeks, or months. They have learned from the culture that women wear dresses, even though their experience at home may be contrary. It is a mystery why girls in that stage of development think that being female borders on looking grotesque. The fuller the dress, shinier the shoes, frillier the frills, the better it is. These girls learned somewhere that a female's looks are of paramount importance. Pretty is crucial. They've learned that women are supposed to be prettier in skirts.

"For months she begged me to wear a dress," reported one mother. "Look pretty, for Daddy, is what she said. I tell her she is pretty all the time — naked, clothed, every way. I hope it has some effect. I understand this phase passes, that when they are about six you can't get them into a dress. I can't wait. It will give me some peace."

One preschooler felt her teacher's rejection of skirts meant that no woman should wear skirts. Her teacher "explained to her that was not so. I told her it was a matter of choice. I am more comfortable in pants and shorts. But I asked her to look at Jane, who wears pants and shorts and skirts."

What do you do when a little girl goes skirt-crazy? Wait for it to pass, but meanwhile find ways of coping. Ask her how she moves differently in a dress than when she is wearing pants. Ask her what she cannot do when she is wearing a skirt. Point out how cool skirts are in the summer, but how cold they are in the winter. Suggest a smock over a pair of pants as a compromise in cold weather. Who are her idols? Maybe her female teacher or babysitter. Observe what those women wear and talk about it. Tell her that clothes you wear, like what you do with your life, is a matter of choice.

Our children learn about life from us, but they also learn a great deal from television and the movies. Much of what they see in advertising and in programming sets up a distorted view of how men and women behave and what they are concerned about. Much of the message is sexist, yet even parents committed to raising non-sexist children are unwilling to ban television watching. After all, TV does teach the children about the culture they live in, and it does afford an in-house entertainment that harried parents of every political persuasion are unwilling to give up.

The *Surgeon General's Report of 1972* and other investigations have demonstrated that children learn pro- and anti-social behavior by observing televised models. Television may also be teaching sex-role behavior. In 1976, three City University of New York students set out to document how men and women are portrayed on television. Cecilia Perez, Bonni R. Seegmiller, and Dorothy Ranier studied television commercials over a four-month period on three network and two local stations at all hours of the day and night. For the morning hours when young children would be likely to be looking at television, they recorded and analyzed 349 commercials.

Of the 908 characters in the 349 commercials, 60 percent were male and 40 percent were female. In more than half the commercials a voice-of-authority narrator was heard. Female narrators were heard 8 percent of the time, male narrators 92 percent. The women's voices were heard in commercials aimed exclusively at women. Twice as many men as women gave product information to others. Women characters were dominated far more often than men characters; women were criticized much more frequently; but men dispensed praise more often than women. Although both sexes were seen as competent, women were only skilled in using products stereotypically used by housewives. Females displayed 82 percent of the nurturant behavior. Only men were aggressive.

The numbers found in this survey substantiate what we already know about television — that it tells viewers that women are inordinately concerned with cleanliness. "I was *proud* of that floor," exclaims one commercial housewife. "Television is the worst purveyor of models in our culture," comments one psychiatrist. "There's always somebody — a woman in an apron — talking about rings on shirts, or taking care of husband and family. There are some attempts to sound liberated. Like, 'I work a full day and then I take care of my kids.' That misses the whole point. The constant shining of floors and dishes with a woman constantly worried about that is insidious. The kids, even in a community where most women have careers, pick that up. To them it is important."

There is an assumption on the part of the advertising world that mother is in charge of health care and nutrition for the whole family. "Mommy makes them feel better with medicines from Bayer" tells a small girl that she'll be in charge of health in her family when she is an adult. Birdseye vegetables are what "your wife can prepare for you," as if boiling several tablespoons of water and salt, then heating frozen vegetables is necessarily tied to skills determined by gender.

Television commercials tell children what is important to the sexes. In a Yuban coffee ad the woman is defined by the quality coffee she makes. Horrors, her husband will take a second cup of another woman's coffee, but never takes a second cup of hers. The ad, of course, never questions the basic assumption that coffee making is a female job, or opens up the possibility that a person who drinks coffee of an inferior variety might say, straight out, to the coffee maker, "Gee, I don't like this coffee. What's wrong?" Secrecy about coffee making and heaven knows what else between the sexes is sustained by the commercials. In other commercials, the women are nearly orgasmic over the shine on their dishes/floors/counter tops. He is appreciative how soft her hands feel.

There is also a trend on the part of Madison Avenue and their cohorts to co-opt the women's movement and make money out of their pockets. Pampers has run a print ad that says the future President of the United States deserves a drier bottom. This baby wears a pink romper and has bows in her hair. A set of Inglenook wine ads on radio and television evoke a similar response. Inglenook is a quality California wine I buy because it is good, but I am more disposed to buy that wine because of their advertisements. One radio ad toasts the arrival of a new baby. "Here's to the new baby," says the male announcer, "The future President of the United States. Here's to Debbie." Another Inglenook television and radio ad records the opening of wine to celebrate graduation from medical school. The father offers a toast, "to my daughter, the doctor." "I wanted to be a cheerleader and you said, 'Be the head of the squad.' I wanted to go into medicine and you said, 'Be a doctor,'" says the new female doctor about her father and his encouragement. During the ad my eyes tear up, maybe my ears do too; I'm not sure these quotes are exact. Although advertisers are more than willing to size up the feminist market and exploit it, there is the possibility that more women in more advertising agencies are changing the way women are portrayed in print, on radio, and on television.

Television commercials are only a part of the battle. Most parents have a quarrel with children's programming also. "Our daughter doesn't watch much television. 'Mr. Rogers' is the show we tend to like best. 'Sesame Street' is too fast, requires a low concentration," said one father. "The television my kids watch is the same dumb stuff," says another father. " 'Jeannie' is a dumb show and a dumb witch. 'That Girl' — Marlo Thomas acts dumb, but so does the man."

"My son asked me to look at the show 'Adam 12.' 'The cops were so nice, Mom,' he said. 'Well,' I told him, 'I wish you would watch the eleven o'clock news. The police were beating up people,' " said a mother concerned about the seeming reality television teaches her son.

"I see television messing up these kids the same way it messed us up," said a preschool teacher. "All these shows about men who are stronger and hostile. It's very hard to undo all that is built into them away from school. The TV, movies . . . the Walt Disney films . . . all the female characters are terrible models."

"Why are the 'Flintstones,' the 'Bionic Woman,' 'Adam 12' the most popular shows?" asks a day-care director. "It is because the shows are about power. The power children do not have. The girls like *Bewitched* because it is about power, too. This lovely blonde creature with so much power chooses to use it only around home, family, and children."

Action for Children's Television is a group that advises parents to treat television with tender loving care. They offer a set of guidelines to help parents use television as a tool in their children's lives: "Talk about TV with your child! Talk about programs that delight your child. Talk about programs that upset your child. Talk about the differences between make-believe and real life. Talk about ways TV characters could solve problems without violence. Talk about violence and how it hurts. Talk about TV foods that can cause cavities. Talk about TV toys that may break too soon.

"Look at TV with your child! Look out for TV behavior

your child might imitate. Look for TV characters who care about others. Look for women who are competent in a variety of jobs. Look for people from a variety of cultural and ethnic groups. Look for healthy snacks in the kitchen instead of on TV. Look for ideas for what to do when you switch off the set . . . read a book . . . draw a picture . . . play a game.

"Choose TV programs with your child! Choose the number of programs your child can watch. Choose to turn the set off when the program is over. Choose to turn on public television. Choose to improve children's TV by writing a letter to a local station . . . to a television network . . . to an advertiser . . . to Action for Children's Television." (A full-color, 8½" x 11" TREAT TV WITH T.L.C. poster is available from ACT without charge.)

Toys are the props children use to rehearse for life. As builders of block cities and movers of toy machines, children prepare for lives as architects and city managers, construction workers and taxi drivers. Traditionally boys have been encouraged to create a fantasy world of power in the community and important employment. Girls have been restricted to re-creating the home environment in their play.

Nobody asked me at the age of four if I had the manual dexterity or desire to learn how to iron. But my father lovingly fashioned a wooden iron, painted it silver to simulate metal, and equipped me with an ironing board. I set about to practice my sex-appointed task of ironing. Who knew if my brother had more of an aptitude for smoothing shirt collars and setting pants' creases? He was out, busy with his coaster wagon, while I set up my ironing board. I was given an iron because I was a girl. I practiced to do like Mama. I was given toys so that I could be a houseworker-in-training.

Commercial toy makers have been in league with the stereotypes-that-be to train little girls to assume their houseworker role later in life. The Little Suzy Homemaker line of toys scales household appliances down to child size. Battery power tones down the voltage so girl children who practice cooking and caring and cleaning risk only burns, not electrocution. Irons, blenders, ovens, sinks, and other labor-learning devices are readily available. Currently there is a line of Holly Hobbie appliances advertised to little girls. Set in some imprecise but nonetheless nostalgic age of gingham dresses, flounced skirts, and quilts, the Holly Hobbie series romanticizes household chores. There is a Holly Hobbie sewing machine on the market which is advertised to encourage girls to sit by the hearth, with a cat on the rug, and sew clothes for the family.

"I will not buy my daughter a sweeper and a dustpan. That's one way the women's movement has touched me. A few years ago I would have bought her a cleaning set in a minute. Now I won't," said one mother.

"Whenever I pick up Alison at the Y, she is standing at a toy sink washing dishes. She loves that sink and whenever she sees it on television, she gets excited. Should I buy it for her for Christmas? I really don't know what to do. Dishes are a part of real life. She sees me do them. I guess I should reinforce the opposite, but I don't know what is right," worried another mother.

"My mother gave Kate a toy blender and it is her favorite toy. She will make milk shakes every chance she gets. I won't deprive her of the blender, but I don't want her to practice being the woman-in-the-kitchen, either."

Psychoanalyst Erik H. Erikson observed that girls at play emphasize *inner* space, while boys stress *outer* space. Their play is a function of their anatomy. He observed 150 girls and 150 boys three times each over the period of two years. Girls created interior scenes because of their own inner space, their wombs, he concluded. Boys built large projectiles and composed exterior, active scenes.

Erikson explains the difference in play by comparing the bodies of the children. He doesn't address the socialization of the different sexes, nor does he consider sexism. After all, *Identity: Youth and Crisis* was published in 1968, before the women's movement had made much impact on the national consciousness. Another factor that would influence the difference between the girls' play and the boys' play were the toys and figures they used. The human figures he used in his observation are not illustrated, but there is very good chance the female figures could only be used in interior scenes, since until very recently the block figures available were painted into sterotypic and limited roles. In a set of figures the female was most often a nurse, or a mother. The adult women figures were drawn holding babies, mixing bowls, or wearing aprons, thereby making it impossible to put those women figures in an exterior setting.

Children and adults have trouble fantasizing themselves as characters of a different sex. Now non-stereotyped, multiracial figures are on the market. The females can be outdoors or in; the males' arms are free of newspapers so they can hug children. Educator Barbara Sprung reports in her book *Non-Sexist Education for Young Children* the delight one eight-year-old girl expressed when she saw the new, non-stereotyped figures. She said, "Oh, this will make pretending much easier."

Parents and educators who want to make it easier for children to pretend to be whatever they dream of being are fighting an ingrained notion that toys are either girls' toys or boys' toys. A clerk in a toy store found that out the hard way. "I always used to ask how old the child was and then I would suggest toys. One time I said that Lego would be a good present for a four year old. The woman nearly bit my head off. 'No, it is a girl.' I think she bought a doll." Girls' toys, to that customer and to others, are narrowly confined to the doll/home/crafts sphere. Boys' toys are a much wider range, taking in everything *but* doll/home/crafts.

Children are very careful to play with toys considered appropriate to their gender. In *The Psychology of Sex Differences*, Eleanor Emmons Maccoby and Carol Nagy Jacklin report studies that children are prone to play with toys they've been told are appropriate for their sex. Girl children had more freedom to play with boys' toys, but boy children felt restrained from playing with girls' toys when the boys thought someone was watching. Seemingly unobserved, the boys played with the girls' toys.

Blocks and lincoln logs are among the toys labeled "male." They teach important lessons about gravity and proportion and fractions that every child should learn. A child who doesn't practice balancing blocks at age three is going to be lousy at spatial relations at ten, fifteen, and thirty. Traditionally boys have practiced with and learned from blocks from a very early age.

Another exclusively male province has been guns and war toys. One psychiatrist commented, "Toy soldiers are played with differently than Fisher-Price people." Boys act out aggression and domination and death. Feminist parents of boys and girls would like to see war toys eliminated, but face a struggle. "For a long time Russell went around shooting everyone with his finger. I finally asked him what he wanted for Christmas. He wanted a toy gun, so we got him one. But first we talked about it at length. What guns are used for. How they are made. What people do with guns. Russell used to say, 'I would only use my gun to shoot an animal, and only if I needed the food.' That was pretty heavy for a kid, but he grasped how serious guns are. He slowly got into the peer group play with guns, but they are not the biggest thing to him, which might have been if we handled it differently," said a mother.

"We just will not buy toy guns. We won't spend our money on them. Johnnie got one as a present and immediately threw it out to please us. I picked it out of the trash and told him he didn't have to do that. Eventually he decided to throw it away, but he had to get the gun thing out of his system. He knows they kill, but they were fascinating to him," said another parent.

When some people hear about non-sexist parenting they immediately think — dolls for boys and trucks for girls and you are on your way to creating a non-sexist child. It ain't necessarily so, but dolls do play an important part in teaching young children how to be nurturant parents.

There are a number of attractive and anatomically realistic boy dolls on the market now. They are in the fifteen to twenty dollar price range, which puts them out of reach for a good number of families, but they are made in this country and available in major department stores. For years, baby boy dolls with genitalia were available only by mail. It is not certain if they came in a plain brown wrapper. Parents, for some reason, have never anguished about giving girls dolls with nothing between their legs. They fear little boys would think something had been cut off. Don't they realize little girls might check out the obvious difference between the doll and themselves, and reach the very same frightening conclusion?

Feminist Selma Greenberg is against dolls. "A doll just lies there," she says. "A doll is no preparation for motherhood. Babies move. Dolls don't. Let the kid nurture a frog, even, a dog, a kitten, a gerbil. The animal is alive."

"Even when we give boys dolls we hand it to them differently. At arm's length you give a boy a doll. But a little girl, you cuddle the doll and hand it to her gently," said another feminist. "They do different things with the dolls, because we do different things with them."

The Public Action Coalition on Toys (PACT) has set as its goal the development of quality toys and the elimination of toys that injure, exploit, or limit a child's growth. Some of the injury and limitation are in the form of sexism. PACT makes annual awards to specific toys that fulfill their guidelines.

The PACT guidelines for choosing toys are the following: Look for toys that are safe, lasting, and marked non-poisonous. Don't buy toys with sharp edges or points; dolls or stuffed animals with wires or buttons; powerful toys, such as gas- or electric-powered rockets or cars; pellet guns; or glass mirrors. Look for realistic dolls that portray racial as well as individual variations with dignity.

Avoid toys that equate self-concept with acquiring material goods, such as dolls that demand limitless accessories and outfits. Look for toys that provide non-sexist, multi-ethnic role models, such as a black woman doctor, or a man caring for children. Don't buy toys that encourage sadism or glorify militarism; avoid guns, monsters, war toys, fighting toys, torture or horror kits. Avoid craft kits that can be easily and more cheaply duplicated. Look for toys that pique a child's creativity and lend themselves to a number of play situations. Remember, a good toy is for a girl *or* a boy.

Toys are the tools of childhood. If children are forbidden from imagining themselves in one role or another in play, how can they possibly imagine themselves in that role in real life. Present children with all the choices, and then let them choose according to personality, not sex, what they envision for themselves in fantasy and in reality.

11

THE MALE BIAS OF THE MOTHER TONGUE

 MALE bias to our
mother tongue is evident from the very beginning of life.
"Papa" or "Dada" is supposed to be baby's first word. When it
is not, sometimes there is worry. One mother even reported
that when her baby boy's first word was "Mama," her husband
was upset and said, "He's going to be a sissy."

Children in this country learn what used to be called the
King's English. Now the language belongs to the common
man, but not yet to the common woman. Our usage of the
English language should be changed because it is sexist and
exclusionary. It damages developing children. Every child
learning the language starts out with halting attempts to use
pronouns. Each one makes mistakes in the process, but because of the sexual politics of the English language, a girl
child is corrected many more times than a boy.

In her first attempts to use pronouns, a little girl will most
probably refer to everyone and everything with female pronouns. After all, those are the pronouns she hears most frequently whenever anyone talks about her, and since she undoubtedly, if she runs to childlike form, thinks that she is the
center of the universe, she will assume the rest of the world is
"she" and "her" as well.

Soon enough she will find that she is wrong. Everything is
not female. Most things are not female. Even things where
females play an important part, like the entire human race,
are referred to as male. The entire human race, 51 percent of
it women, has been known as "mankind" or, more simply and
more incorrectly, "man."

The girl who tries to expand on her experience and apply it to the language will be corrected time and time again. "The bunny, he, dear," "The bird, he, darling." "Papa is a he, sweetheart." The instructor is right about Papa, but the cricket she caught on the lawn last night, and the toad she let go this morning have as good a chance of being a she (to those of us ignorant in the ways of differentiating between the male and female of those species) as of being a he.

Correct English usage labels the girl's use of pronouns wrong. She is told over and over again that almost everything is male. Since she is part of the female pronoun set, she is excluded. Grammatically she is a non-person. Children cannot and do not grasp the linguistic concept that the specific stands for the general. A two-year-old girl does not know that "Will every child put his toys away?" means her toys, too. She is excluded by the language and made to feel as if she were not there. No wonder little girls are too often quiet and passive and fade into the wall.

When a little boy is learning the language, he more often meets with success and positive reinforcements. Again, like an egocentric little girl, the egocentric little boy thinks he is the center of the world. He assumes everything is male, and like the little girl, makes some mistakes. Mama, for example, is not a he. Neither is the family mutt who delivered a litter of six last week. However, proportionally, the young male linguist is right more often than the young female.

According to the rules of English grammar, the frogs in the pond are male. The pigs in the farm book, male, too. Whenever the sex is questionable, or unknown, or even when females and males are both clearly present in a group, the English language uses a male referent. Extrapolating from his own experience as a male he labels things correctly and is praised.

Male children learn from the language that their own assumptions that the world is male are true. The male child feels included, for he is male, also. There is no need for a boy to process the generic pronoun before he feels included, as every little girl must do. The male generic pronoun states that he is part of the action.

The exclusive use of the male generic pronoun promotes the attitude that women are not an important part of the human race. In childhood, men are never forced to include women in their language and are never encouraged, or forced, as girls are, to read, speak, and hear the English language through a grid that translates it to include both sexes. Males are subliminally told that everything is male. The language says so. They are given a linguistic license to exclude women from the board room, the union hall, from anywhere.

In *A New Guide to Rational Living*, Albert Ellis and Robert A. Harper make what seems on the face of it to be a simplistic statement, but one that has damaging implications for women. Ellis and Harper observe that "practically all of us, by the time we reach adulthood, seem to do most of our important thinking, and consequently our emoting in terms of self-talk or internalized sentences. Humans, as uniquely language-creating animals, begin to learn from early childhood to formulate thoughts, perceptions, and feelings in words, phrases, and sentences. They usually find this easier than to think in pictures, sounds, touch units, or other possible methods." Humans think about themselves in words and sentences. English-speaking females are working with a handicap. They cannot think of themselves in sentences that include them unless the language is altered.

Is English so sacred, so static, that we cannot change its structure to include the sex of more than half the people who speak it? Let us look at the suggested pronouns that include both sexes.

In *The Liberated Man*, Warren Farrell suggests a new set of pronouns. He offers what he calls "human pronouns." *Te*, which is pronounced like *tea*, means *he* or *she* (nominative). *Tes*, which rhymes with *fez*, means *his* or *her* (possessive). *Tir*, which rhymes with *her*, means *him* or *her* (objective). Farrell suggests that human pronouns be used instead of a pronoun that refers to a woman or a man. "Every student is worried about his grades" becomes "Every student is worried about tes grades." Run them around on your tongue a couple of times. The new pronouns are awkward and certainly contrived. But are they unnatural? Who says pronouns that exclude half the race are natural?

If the English-speaking population was committed to eradicating sexism in both word and deed, we could get used to a new set of pronouns. Manufactured words, adapted words, have made it into common usage after a scientific or industrial breakthrough. Some of those are awkward. Certainly *monosodium glutamate* sounds unnatural! We should be able to accommodate a breakthrough in the equality of the sexes by adding three little words to English.

Currently there is no general pronoun revolution on the horizon. No powerful organization of linguists is working to promote equality of pronouns and wipe out the male bias of the English language.

However, the National Council of Teachers of English (NCTE) has encouraged writers to type their way around the deficiencies in the language. They suggest rewriting, whenever possible, the male generic pronoun and the use of words like *man* for *humankind*.

William F. Buckley, Jr., is one writer who takes great umbrage at the NCTE's suggestions, warning that if they are followed, clarity and precision in English writing will be lost. In his newspaper column attacking the guidelines, Buckley doesn't argue the merits of the case — the real sexism of the language. But, in all fairness, Buckley can't know that sexism from experience. He is one man in mankind.

Buckley argues that if "the common man" is rephrased to read "the average person, or ordinary people" the connotations are different. He writes that replacing "the average student is worried about his grades" with "the average student is worried about grades" suggests a student is worried about grades as a philosphical subject, rather than a semester's reality. He claims the substitute is imprecise.

Since Buckley rejects the admittedly awkward "he and she" to replace "he," why not elevate "she" to generic status? Then if "she" was used in alternate sentences with "he," part of the exclusionary problem would be solved. Half the human race would still be omitted, but only in alternate sentences.

It is insensitivity more than anything, I feel, that allows Buckley and others like him to remain rigid on the subject of changing the English language. Buckley doesn't understand "what's inherently sexist about *Libber*" and why *feminist* is a better word choice. He's worried about preserving precise connotations, yet seems not to realize that *Libber* has a pejorative connotation. He doesn't understand why *man-sized job* should be replaced by the words *big* or *enormous job*. He asks, "How do you describe a job that requires physical exertion beyond the biological powers of wopersons?" A job that is beyond the physical strength of "wopersons" would be too great for a number of men as well. Women and men come in different strengths and sizes.

Buckley stands opposed to altering the language to make it more fair. So do many of the men I talked to. Views on changing the language and the importance of that change were divided along sex lines. Women think the language is important and that change is in order. Men, for the most part, shrug their shoulders and are indifferent to any need for changing the sexist politics of the English language. Even some fathers committed to raising non-sexist daughters and sons do not think a language revolution is important.

They are reluctant to admit, or are maybe genuinely naïve about, the benefits they have accrued from speaking and hearing a language that is biased in the direction of their sex. They laugh and say, "What difference does it make? Sexism is so much more." Sexism *is* so much more, but the language is a part of it. If it makes no difference that *he* means *she* as well, then let's use *she* to mean *he*, too. Let the she's have a turn!

Parents can take a political stand about sexism and the language. "Don't use the male pronoun all the time," says the mother of one son emphatically. "The second turtle we got was given a girl's name. I don't know what it is, but we call it her. I thought it was only fair," said a father of two.

Personally, I have extended my politics to the bunnies on the lawn and the land toads and even the dogs of indeterminate sex in the park. I choose to use the female pronoun more than half the time when I refer to the animals. Half the time I am going to be right. I'm allowing myself that more-than-half margin to make up for the male bias around me. Even more important than my own use of the language, I am teaching my daughter to question other people's use of it.

I have often asked Casey if she thinks a particular worker or specific animal is female or male. We question the assumption that all is male. All is not male. She isn't. Now I hear her asking her friends, and herself in the process, what sex a creature is. She does not assume they are male. I consciously flout grammatical rules of male-female order. If women and men are equal, why do the females always trail? In my house, *girls* often come before *boys* in a sentence, *women* before *men*. I cannot change the grammar books single-handedly, but I can help change usage that grammar books will have to reflect someday.

What we have to work with is a highly masculine language. Otto Jespersen, a multilingual Dane, examined our language and wrote *The Growth and Structure of the English Lanugage*. He claims that English is "the most positively and expressively masculine" of all the languages he knows. To him, English is "the language of a grown-up man, with very little childish or feminine about it." He says its best qualities are its terseness, logicality, freedom from pedantry, openness to innovation, and emotional restraint. Jespersen labels these qualities masculine, and considers effusiveness, long-windedness, ebullience, and adherence to the status quo to be "childish and feminine" or "childlike and effeminate." Jespersen treats "childish" and "feminine" as synonyms.

Three major American publishing houses have taken a critical look at the language. Finding their own publications and stylebooks rife with sexist language, they each have developed guidelines for fair treatment of females and males in their products. The guidelines, in pamphlet form, can be obtained by writing for "Guidelines for Equal Treatment of the Sexes in McGraw-Hill Book Company Publications" (this is the best of the three); or "Guidelines for the Development of Elementary and Secondary Instructional Materials — the Treatment of Sex Roles," Holt, Rinehart and Winston, Inc., School Department; or "Guidelines for Improving the Image of Women in Textbooks" from Scott, Foresman and Company.

These guidelines are useful for parents who need help talking and writing without a sexist bias. I sometimes listen to myself speaking very slowly and haltingly to children. It is not that they can't hear well or think quickly, it's that I'm so cautious about what I might blurt out. As I try to replace "mailman" with "letter carrier," or use alternate-sex single pronouns in alternate sentences, once in a while my speaking pace slows or is broken by silences while I edit. These publishing guidelines have helped me pick up the pace.

All three suggest avoiding the generic use of the male pronoun, and insist that when *he* is intended to mean both sexes, its inclusive meaning should be explicitly explained. They suggest alternating between male and female expressions whenever possible. They also support rewording of sentences. For example: "The average American child likes his apple juice cold" should be reworded to read "The average American child likes apple juice cold," or recast in the plural, "Most American children like their apple juice cold." I doubt you will be lecturing your child on the apple-juice preferences of fellow country-children, but you get the idea.

The guidelines discourage the use of *man*-words, agreeing that girls and women should be included in titles, examples, and the general language. McGraw-Hill offers the following possible substitutions for *man*-words:

man-word	substitute
mankind	humanity, human race, people
primitive man	primitive people or peoples
man's achievements	human achievements
"If a man drove 50 miles . . ."	"If a person (or driver) drove 50 . . ."
the best man for the job	the best person (or candidate)
man-made	synthetic, artificial, manufactured
manpower	human energy, workforce
grow to manhood	grow to adulthood, manhood, or womanhood

Another frontier for the language is relabeling jobs so they apply to workers of both sexes. The last few years *person* has been the official non-sexist suffix. There are other alternatives. Even the U.S. Department of Labor's Manpower Division has renamed occupations to remove sexism. The division has not renamed itself, however. Holt, Rinehart and Winston suggest the following reassignments. You can devise your own non-sexist descriptive terms.

Sexist titles	Non-sexist job titles
policeman	police officer
fireman	firefighter
workman	worker
repairman	plumber, electrician, etc.
chairman	chairperson or chair
caveman	cave dweller
congressman, congresswoman	Member of Congress
businessman	business person
mailman	postal worker, letter carrier
insurance man	insurance agent

The pamphlet warns, "Be careful to avoid using *-person* coinages to mean *woman* as in 'Chairman George Smith and Chairperson Louise Brown' or 'The salesmen and other salespeople in the Western Region.'" Men are people, too.

Adjectives often connote attitude. Men are usually described by how they function, and women are described by how they look. For example, "Jeff is smart. Sally is pretty." It is important to describe parallel qualities. If you describe her red hair, you'd better mention his bald pate. Sometimes that means listening carefully and not saying what comes naturally.

"I was soothing this upset, snotty-faced, ratty-haired little girl," said one preschool teacher, "when I heard myself say, 'Let's wash your face and fix your hair so you'll look nice for Daddy.' From what part of my brain did that come? Some old part, some recess. I was telling that little girl she should look pretty, no matter how she felt. I sighed and rephrased for function. 'Let's wash your face and fix your hair so you'll feel better.'"

Children learn about themselves from the words they hear. A good self-image develops out of a positive vocabulary. If we want to raise girl children who consider themselves complete human beings who count, then we'd better speak a language that treats women as equals. If we want to raise boy children who respect women and who won't think that being a man is the only thing to be, we should stop speaking a language that reinforces sexism.

12

BOOKS CAN BE FRIENDS

MY generation was taught that "books are your friends" and we were admonished, for that reason, not to write in them, rip them, dirty them, or question the message they sent us. But for the women of the fifties and sixties, books were not our friends. They were our enemies, accomplices in the evil task of undermining the equality of the sexes and of teaching us our place.

Dick and Jane and Spot and Puff in our school readers taught us what was expected of female children and adults in the mid-twentieth century. Girls were to watch and wait, while the boys were to be active.

In 1970, Women on Words and Images, in Princeton, New Jersey, organized to study sex role stereotyping in school readers. They discovered that textbooks were filled with pictures of girls who were afraid and passive, and boys who were fearless and invincible. The fathers were only breadwinners and mothers were only housewives. The group examined the contents of readers published by fourteen major publishing houses, then created "Dick and Jane as Victims: Sex Stereotyping in Children's Readers," a booklet and slide show, to illustrate their findings.

What did the study group discover in the 2,760 stories read in the 134 books? That boys are better, more numerous, and stronger. The statistics show that boys and men are seen in greater numbers than women and girls. In some of the books, girls are only minor characters. No series of readers had an equal number of girl and boy stories.

Boy-centered stories outweighed girl-centered stories five

to two. Adult male main characters outnumbered adult female main characters three to one. In biographies, male lives were told six to one over female. Even the animal kingdom came across as sexist. Two to one, the male animal characters outnumbered the female.

Women characters were seen almost without exception as mother, housekeeper, nurse, telephone operator, and teacher, as well as a few other stereotypic lower-level workers. Male characters, however, could do anything. They were seen in six times as many jobs as the female characters.

Girls were depicted as wistful and tentative, while boys were positive and energetic. Take for example a page from Harper and Row's *City Days, City Ways* (1966) that shows a little girl sitting on a stoop, petting the dog at her feet, while she leans her chin on her hand and stares off into space. "What can I do?" asks the caption. Given her body position and the listless look on her face, the best thing she could do would be to get a vitamin B-12 shot. But this child doesn't even think of that. She is without initiative and creativity. Contrast her with an illustration from *My City,* a Bank Street Reader by the Macmillan Company (1966). The same words caption the picture, but in a different order. "What I can do" proclaims the little boy, who in the picture is standing on his head, his cap on his foot, whistling. What confidence, what ingenuity this boy child has.

Children get a sense of themselves from the repetition of images in the books that they read. Sexist attitudes that are repeated over and over again in books and in the media slowly alter their perceptions until stereotypes and myths about men and women are accepted as reality.

Consider the long-term effect of illustrations showing a little girl, her hands clasped around her back, watching an active boy. Such illustrations have an effect on the development of both sexes. School readers tell children what is expected of them and they give children a picture of what they assume is the real world.

In the readers, girls were constantly belittled and denigrated. In the Harper and Row book, *Trade Winds,* "Oh, Raymond, boys are much braver than girls," states straight out that girls are fearful. A Lippincott reader, *Book H* (1970), says that even when they grow up, girls will be of little value: "Women's advice is never worth two pennies. Yours isn't worth even a penny." The readers at every point reinforce the stereotype that girls are vain, housedrudges, fearful, unimaginative, and not very smart.

With the growth of the women's movement, and a "women's market" for books, you would think that publishers would edit their textbooks with an eye toward profit as well as fairness. That has not been the case. Women on Words and Images updated their survey of readers in 1975, examining the books published since 1972.

It was by and large difficult to get the new materials from the publishers. A few refused to participate, mentioning scheduled revisions of their readers. Others sent their company policies or guidelines on sexism.

The eighty-three sample books reviewed continued the gross imbalance of male-to-female ratios. Although publishers had added a few more girl-centered stories, male still ran ahead seven to two. Male illustrations were twice as numerous, and males had three times as many jobs to pick from as females.

Publishing houses are being simultaneously pressured to erase both sexism and racism from their publications. Too often, sexist ideas are repeated when a book is revised to reflect our multi-racial world. In the 1966 version of Harper and Row's *Around the Corner,* Mark says, "She is just like a girl. She gives up." The 1972 version puts the same sexist statement in the mouth of Pedro.

Are you pleased with the texts your children are using? Do they depict life as it really is, or some limited picture of how people should live? If you feel your children's books are setting boys and girls into narrowly defined sex roles, which are insulting to girls and harmful to both sexes, there are many things you can do to effect change.

Become your own public relations outfit, even if there are only two of you. Have stationery printed. Give yourselves a name. Groups do get more attention than a single person.

Write letters to the editors of your local papers and local radio stations about the quality of instructional material in the school system. Encourage the media to cover sexism in the textbooks and in the school system.

Lobby for attention from the board of education and the state legislature. Pressure for legislation that would prohibit sex-role stereotyped material in the public schools. Write to your member of Congress and your Senators as well.

At this time at least three states, California, Iowa, and New Jersey, have legislated against sex-biased school supplies. State boards of education in Colorado, Maryland, New Jersey, South Dakota, and West Virginia have proposed or passed resolutions against sex-biased materials.

Feminists fighting for such legislation may meet resistance from people who believe that rules about reading and teaching materials are unconstitutional — a denial of the First Amendment right of free speech. But state and local officials are already routinely reviewing and choosing textbooks. Feminists are asking these judges to adopt standards and avoid selecting sex-biased materials.

Even before any legislation or resolutions are passed, you can meet with the people who select texts, either on a state or local level, and share your point of view. Sometimes individual teachers are responsible for picking the books. Let those with the power know your concern about sexism. Offer to meet with them, talk about the issues, and search for non-biased materials.

Once a school, or school system, is committed to rejecting sex-biased materials, it can exert its influence. Letters on official stationery can go to every publishing house announcing the school system's intention of rejecting any and all materials that do not meet certain non-sexist criteria. You can either draw up your own guidelines, or send along some put together by one of the publishing houses or a feminist group. Perhaps you could send along a copy of the "Dick and Jane as Victims" pamphlet, with salient parts underlined and asterisked.

Write to editors in publishing houses about specific books

or stories that please you, or offend you. Be specific. Try to offer alternatives.

Changing textbooks is slow and expensive. Since it takes at least two years for the writing, production, and printing of a textbook, sexism will not be erased from those readers overnight. Even the companies that profess a commitment to change are quick to point out the costs are staggering. The Women's Equity Action League education kit reports that "it takes half a million dollars to launch a new series and five years to get that series from writer to child."

Because texts are often inappropriate, many teachers and schools are no longer relying as heavily upon them. Instead, paperback books for all levels of readers are in popular use. Outfits like The Feminist Press (Old Westbury, New York) and Lollipop Power, Inc. (Chapel Hill, North Carolina) among others offer alternative books.

Check out your local and school libraries to see if there is a good selection of role-free books and books about women. Talk with the librarians and urge them to order non-sexist books, biographies of women, and women's magazines like *Ms.* and *Womansports*.

In the same year that Women on Words and Images started its work on school readers, another group formed and began compiling a bibliography of quality books about females for young readers. A number of women in New York, upset by the stereotyped picture of girls and women in children's books, formed Feminists on Children's Media. Believing that strict sex-role stereotyping harms young readers as they develop, Feminists on Children's Media studied a wide range of children's books, then undertook to enlighten publishers, writers, teachers, librarians, and parents about the problem of sexism in children's literature.

The group presented to a meeting of the Author's Guild and the Children's Book Council in October 1970 a lecture program with slides from children's books. The slides, including some pictures that are part of the "Dick and Jane as Victims" slide show, illustrated dramatically how differently female and male characters are treated in children's books.

Girls play house, or cry, or wait. Boys build tree houses, play firefighter, and protect girls. A good number of the professionals at that 1970 meeting reported they were not aware how commonplace stereotypes were in children's literature. They resolved to change that.

Feminists on Children's Media also published *Little Miss Muffet Fights Back* a bibliography of recommended books about girls for young readers. After examining more than a thousand recommended titles about intelligent, interesting girls and women, 200 books were included in the bibliography. In three years, without money for advertising or promotion, 25,000 copies of the bibliography were sold. In 1974, Feminists on Children's Media published an updated version.

The books selected for *Little Miss Muffet Fights Back* show women and girls as complete human beings — creative, adventurous, brave, active, clever, and assertive. They are books that illustrate some understanding of social conditions that will help promote self-fulfillment for the reader. Some of the books point out the forces that keep women from becoming all they might be. The list isn't a compilation of stories about saints or superwomen. Nor do the stories follow a feminist "line." The list offers books that reflect life and people in variety.

Feminists on Children's Media has had to defend publishing a bibliography about females instead of about females and males. They considered drawing up a bibliography about boys, listing books that break through the male stereotypes, but the idea was rejected. Books about boys so far outnumber books about girls that the sheer volume was too much for the group to wade through. As it is, the *Miss Muffet* bibliography is for young readers, not for one sex reader or the other. A good book about a girl can be loved by both sexes. *The Wizard of Oz* and *Harriet the Spy* are only two examples of books with girl central characters which have universal appeal.

Accused of pushing feminist "propaganda" for children with its "one-sided list," Feminists on Children's Media were quick to point out that books for children in the libraries and bookstores are neither neutral nor do they reflect life as it really is. Research proves that the real world is very different from the world of children's books. For example, almost half the women in this country work outside the home. Few women in children's books have jobs or careers. Those who work in the home only faintly resemble the real variety which is involved in community, school, or church work.

Little Miss Muffet Fights Back is a fine source for parents and teachers to use in developing a library of role-free books, but there are also other more recent lists available. *The Liberty Cap*, a bimonthly journal of recently published, non-stereotyped children's books and resources, is published in Palo Alto, California. Academy Press has put out *Guide to Non-Sexist Children's Books*, a source for more than 400 non-sexist books for preschoolers through twelfth graders. It is a compact guide to building new collections at home or in libraries. Also, *Ms.* Magazine periodically prints an annotated bibliography of new books for free children.

Because we have a tradition in this country that frowns on book burning, the sexist books that are on the shelves are here to stay and the children are going to read them. It is therefore important that children be taught to know sexism *when* they read it. Then a child's consciousness will be raised by a sexist book, not warped by it.

You can't always tell a sexist book by its cover, but sometimes you can. What follows are guidelines you can use, alone or with your child, to evaluate whether or not a children's book is sexist. The criteria are adapted from a checklist developed by The Council on Interracial Books for Children.

1. Look at the copyright date. Only in the last five years have children's books begun to reflect feminist concerns. A book from the late sixties or earlier is more likely to reflect sexism than a newer book. The lag of more than a year between writing and publication of a book meant little in more static times, but in these more volatile times, a four-year-old book can be ancient history.

2. Look at the cover and the illustrations. Are the females passive and the males active? Look out for stereotypes. Are

the women housebound? Do they wear aprons? Are the girls petite and quiet and clean? Is there a wicked stepmother? Are the characters denigrated because of sex?

3. Examine the story line. What is the role of women? Could the same story be told with reversed sex roles? How do the women characters achieve? Is it because of their good looks and their relationship to males? Is it because of their creativity and intelligence? Are sex roles important to the characterization and the story?

What are the standards for success? Must females adopt male behavior patterns of competition and aggression to succeed?

How are the problems solved? Is the oppression of women in society explained, or merely accepted? Is the oppression explained as a result of an unjust society?

4. Look at the way people live. Is the two-child, two-parent white family in suburbia a norm to which every other way of life compares unfavorably? Do mothers and fathers work outside the home? Do both work inside the home? Are there any single or divorced parents? Are differing lifestyles treated as aberrant ways of life?

5. Look at the way people relate. Do the men in the story have all the power? Are the women supportive and serving only? Do the characters show respect for children?

6. Consider the effects on the child's self-image. Are the ideas in the book limiting for one sex or the other? What effect would a book filled with weak and timid females and strong males have on a girl's self-image? Is there at least one strong character with which the child can identify?

7. Who is the writer or artist. Look at his or her qualifications. A book about the thoughts or feelings of a girl that is written by a man should be carefully examined. What are the writer's cultural biases that may be subtly present in the book?

8. Check out the language. Is the singular male pronoun used to refer to both males and females? Is the generic use of the word "man" avoided by using non-sexist language? For example, mail carrier should replace mailman. Letter carrier

is even better, for it replaces the aural "mail" with "letter."
Does the language in the book ridicule or denigrate women?

With these guidelines in mind, you can scan a book and determine whether or not it is sexist. A non-sexist book does not
necessarily mean it is a good one, however. There are some
books on the market that are clearly pandering to the wom-
en's market. Books that are little more than heavy-handed
propaganda should be recognized for what they are.

Occasionally books teach a feminist lesson at the expense of
other human values. *Nice Little Girls,* written by Elizabeth Levy
and published in 1974 by Delacorte, is one such book. It is the
tale of Jackie, a girl who wants to build boxes with hammer,
nails, and wood in her new classroom. Her teacher, Mrs.
James, tells her over and over what nice little girls don't do.
Although Jackie is taunted for acting like a boy, and os-
tracized by all the children, she is a spunky kid, has supportive
parents, and triumphs. All the kids realize girls and boys have
a lot more in common than they had been told.

Hurrah for cutting through sex-role stereotyping! The
trouble with this book, though, is the character of the teacher.
Mrs. James is a jerk, as cardboard and as stereotyped as im-
aginable. She is allowed no humanity. Must there always be a
trade off?

Stuck with inadequate materials, many parents and
teachers cope by first pointing out to the children the errors
or the sexist thinking in the books, then they sit down and
edit.

"We are teaching kids how to live in a culture that is sexist,"
said one preschool teacher. "So when we read to the children
we change the words. It says policeman, I say policeman or
policewoman. I think it is worth the extra words to show the
child she can be that, too."

"We change the pictures," reported another early-
childhood educator. "Picture changing isn't something that
should be happening in the back room. If a book has a picture
of a boy doing something, we will often, as a class, cut out a

picture of a girl and paste it onto the page. You should always say, 'Look here, men and women can do this.' By having the kids help it helps them learn the culture as it is. It is important not to hide kids from what is going on. Certainly if what there is is rotten, you must prepare a kid to deal with it."

"There are only seven or eight books you can use," complained one teacher of preschoolers. "I think a school should make the books. There is not a huge market for the kind of non-sexist book that supports a child's lifestyle and offsets the media. My son, Russell, and I made books. We took a camera and made a book about us. I am black, Russell's father is white, Russell is a mixture.

"After you've made a book, or edited one to your taste, go into the classroom, talk to your child's teacher, and offer to read the book to the class.

"Then talk about sexism with the kids. Talk about differences. Sexism and racism are a function of people not understanding that being different means being different. It does not mean being better.

"One winter day when Russell was little he took off his hat. His hair stood straight up. I was there with the children and said, 'Look at Russell's hair. It is kinky and soft and when the static electricity gets into it, it stands straight up. Look at the difference between his kinky hair and your flat hair. Feel the difference.' They didn't laugh or make fun. They learned that different is different. That time I guess Russell was the book."

One involved father reported an expensive lesson he learned about sexism in books. "I got a list from someone at the college, went right into the bookstore, and ordered them all. Thirty-eight dollars-worth! I brought them home. Oh, my God! The sexist books! I was appalled. I crossed out words. Changed things. What emerged was that you should talk about children in books, not boys and girls. Then you can use he and she. Children should see themselves first as children. Adults should see themselves primarily as people. The books do not talk that way."

"I'm very careful about the books that I buy," said one mother, "but I can't control what other people bring into my house. My own mother gave my daughter a book about a ballerina. I couldn't believe it. Nothing about what a hard life dancers have. Nothing about the training, the sweating, the pain. The book was all tutus and stage makeup!"

"I will only spend my money on books with strong girl characters. I don't even like to buy boy-animal stories for my daughter. It matters what the sex is of the characters she reads about," offered another mother.

"I can't get my older daughter to pretend she is a boy character in a book. It proves to me the need for strong girl characters. She is sex identified. She refuses to be a boy, even in her imagination. But she has no trouble being Frances the badger, Pippi Longstocking, or Dorothy in *The Wizard of Oz*," observed a mother.

One feminist whose children are grown says that she would throw out fairy tales if she had the power. "They are a bad influence. Look at Snow White and Sleeping Beauty. They are not sleeping; they are dead. The Prince comes along in both stories and kisses a corpse. Snow White and Sleeping Beauty should get up and call the cops. It is insane that that is seen as romantic."

The women who are raising daughters and sons today grew up when sexism was very much a reality, but an unnamed and unidentified reality. Since they were not taught to identify, compensate for, or screen out sexism as they read, they grew up thinking there was something wrong with *them*, not with the books.

"When I was a kid and read all those books about electrical engineers, etc., — all those men — I would say, 'Well, that's me. That's me.' Then I thought there was something wrong with me. I thought, 'I guess I'm not really like other women. They are weak. They don't want to do anything. I want to play stoop ball.' I still see the same thing. The girls are passive," says a mother of three.

Another mother was complaining about the books she had

read as a child. There were exciting biographies about men, but "the only biography I ever had in school about a woman was the story of Helen Keller. I was really sorry I wasn't blind, deaf, and dumb. Then I might have had a chance."

A book that made a little girl sorry she wasn't blind, deaf, and dumb was an enemy, not a friend.

13

WHY JOANNA CAN'T DO CALC—
SEXISM IN THE SCHOOLS

AT a West Side Manhattan meeting scores of parents listened attentively to representatives from almost a dozen private and public schools who had come to sell their schools as the place to send children aged five through eighteen.

There in the bastion of liberalism where, you would think, feminists are active and a non-sexist education is available, not one representative of any school even mentioned sexism, its existence or the struggle against it, until a question was raised from the floor. Only two school spokespeople addressed the needs of the *child* or the *student*. Every other speaker talked about the student as *he*. Perhaps it is a mistake to assume that New York educators and parents would be hipper, more aware of the language that excludes half its paying student body.

Even though the speakers ignored sexism in their presentations, they over and over again reported on the "ethnic diversity of our student body." Undoubtedly, the black movement, forced school integration, and a basic sense of civil rights and moral decency has elevated ethnic balance to near the top of the list of considerations in New York private schools. However, the sensitivity to creating a non-sexist educational environment and stating it straight out is still far off.

"Whenever we are asked about non-sexist education at our school," observed one representative, "we find the questioner really wants to know, 'What about the girls? What's happening to them?' At our school the education for both boys and girls has changed in the last years. We are being fair to both."

Other school speakers echoed the equality-for-both-sexes de-
fense, somehow uncomfortable with the suspicion that boy
students might be getting the shaft.

One can't help but ask, why are the schools so overly conscious to defend the treatment of the boys, when for years
girls' educations were inferior and narrow? There is no
suggestion here that boys be made to suffer so that girls can
get a fair shake. No revenge is called for. However, there
should be some redress for the crimes against the education
of girls of the past. The schools have some making up to do.

"It is through our courses in ethics that we deal with
sexism," reported one speaker. "We try to get to the children
on a feeling level about the sharing that should go on between
men and women. But we want to help children of both sexes
learn how to compete together, that is one reason why we
have had co-ed gym through the fifth grade."

So co-ed cooking and sewing and woodworking classes have
become standard fare at that school. "The girls in shop class
are really very relaxed," said one visitor. "They are not self-
conscious. It's no big deal." At another school, where sixth
graders can take a Women's Literature course and there are
other attempts to combat sexism, one teacher chose her own
way to cope with boys' cooking. "This one teacher was fla-
grantly sexist," reported one parent, "but I didn't hear about
it until it was over. She separated the boys and girls for cooking. It's as if the sexes eat different kinds of food. What a
Neanderthal attitude!"

At one school, which is all boys kindergarten through
eighth grade and co-ed ninth through twelfth, a proposed
domestic-arts course for the boys met with disapproval. After
the word filtered home that boys were being taught cooking
and sewing skills, the headmaster received an accusatory call
from a parent who charged, "Are you turning them into
fags?"

Two of the schools represented at the Manhattan meeting
were sex-segregated schools. Sex segregation is what some
parents want to buy for their sons. One satisfied mother explained, "This school is more suited to the way boys do things.

Shorter periods of time spent on one subject. Play is rougher and faster. Other schools are more set to the way girls do things than the way boys do them." This woman, speaking about buying the best for her particular child, seemed to implicitly criticize boys who get along well in what she described as a feminine environment. This mother, who proudly described her son's "boyish" qualities and how well his school complemented them, echoed what Patricia Cayo Sexton says in her book, *The Feminized Male*, about the personality of schools in this country.

"Schools are so thoroughly feminine that even the music suits girls better. Songs, for example, tend to appeal to their tastes and are usually too high pitched for boy voices. Most forms of self-expression in schools are similarly suited to girls." Apparently, Sexton ignores boy sopranos, whose vocal range runs higher than girls and women. Like the mother with the "boyish" son, Sexton does not explain just what "their tastes" are. She writes as if we all share a certainty of how boys are different from girls, and how, I am afraid, they are better.

Sexton doesn't seem to accept the possibility that men and boys can have female characteristics, except under specific conditions. If they are aberrant, deviant, or if they have been acted upon by women and altered by them, if they have earned the right to take up certain womanly pursuits by dint of their size or their profession, that is tolerable. Sexton writes about her father, a professional boxer, as being "rather confidently masculine." He did delicate embroidery and wrote poetry. Did he earn the right to two feminine pursuits by boxing? Can a non-athletic man be "confidently masculine" and do needlework?

One divorced father who has custody of his daughter and his son says "the women's movement has allowed me to be proud of my own feminine characteristics, like softness and compassion." He felt those characteristics were out of place when he was growing up. "The nurturing qualities, traditionally labeled female, are in me and I like it. I used to hide them, but not anymore." He thinks they make him a better father.

"What does it mean to be masculine?" asks Sexton. "It means, obviously, holding male values and following male behavior norms . . . it appears that male norms stress values such as courage, inner direction, certain forms of aggression, autonomy, mastery, technological skills, group solidarity, adventures, and a considerable amount of toughness in mind and body . . . What is important is that males be liberated, that they be allowed to be boys and/or to do 'girlish' things, as they choose."

Sexton, along with mental-health professionals, many educators, and the majority of the population, enters personality traits in the masculine column that belong to both sexes. What is her form of bookkeeping? Is courage a credit for males and a debit for females? She advises liberating boys to do "girlish" things when and if they choose. What about the girls? Sexton suggests the schools, and the girls, should be masculinized.

"The schools and all childrearing groups would do better to move their standards much further over in a masculine direction, as a means of stimulating top performance in both sexes . . . If we masculinize the schools, girls may suffer. Probably they will not. Girls need most of the same things as boys — activity, self-determination, group integrity, etc. They just don't need them as badly as boys. Aside from rough sports, nothing is taught in any school that girls cannot learn if they are *expected* to. Chances are they would be much more interested in machines than dolls, in doing things than in sitting still, in the real world than in fairy tales. Whatever boys can do (aside from the obvious things, such as playing rough games) girls probably can do just as well. Set male standards and most girls will probably follow them." Set standards on individual preference, personality, and ability, not on sex, and the schools, the world, would be better.

Apart from Sexton's value judgment that male is better than female, or masculine is better than feminine, she does report accurately that schools are places where more women work than men. According to The Racism/Sexism Resource Center in New York City, preschool teachers are 97.9 percent female, elementary teachers are 84.3 percent female, and of all public school teachers 67 percent are women.

A New England educator said, "The administration is top heavy with men. The curriculum heads for the school district, all are men except one. She is head of libraries! There is an intellectual awareness of the women's movement and the inequalities, but the realities are different." The pattern in her community is repeated all over the country. The Resource Center has found that only 27.8 percent of all elementary-education administrators are women. In elementary schools 21 percent of the principals are female, in high schools the percentage of female principals drops to 3 percent. Less than one percent of all superintendents and less than 5 percent of chief state-school officials are women. *Integrated Education* reported in January–February 1976 that the number of women elementary and secondary principals declined by more than 50 percent over the past seventeen years in the city of New York.

The numbers are depressing. The mass of women workers in education have been passed over. Male teachers move up in the ranks to positions of power as principals, curriculum heads, department heads, and superintendents. Sexton claims the men in education are feminized males, men who can't make it in a more masculine world. One high-school teacher wouldn't label the male teachers she has knows as "feminized" or "masculine," but she did say "most of them are jerks."

Male teachers do move up. The statistics are borne out by experience. A male principal always got up in assembly to announce who got honors, who died, the name of the distinguished speaker, as well as the sad news that the movie projector broke again. The female assistant or vice principal sat to his right.

No matter what the breakdown of sexes is in the front office, in the classroom the children are most often in the power of, under the guidance of, women. "The fact that the kids have all women teachers, I find disturbing," commented one parent. "The model of early education is not mixed. They do not have the opportunity to mix with different sexes in different experiences. In the last few years I've seen a shifting focus of what mothers and fathers do, but it is not reflected in the schools."

There are men in the preschool education work force. Newsmagazines and newspapers report about the female and male faculties at day-care centers, at the Montessori schools, and the local nursery schools. However, the articles lead us to believe there are more male pre-primary teachers than there really are. According to the Racism/Sexism Resource Center, the percentage of men in preschool teaching is only 2.1.

From the first group or school experience, a child is in the care of a female. This fact has dire implications for the chance of changing sex roles in our society. "As long as the teacher is a mother replacement, children will continue to expect the female sex to act as caretaker, server, disciplinarian," said one woman.

Parents and teachers trying to break the cycle of experience, expectation, and repetition of traditional sex roles find themselves frustrated. "Okay, I do a lot of the caretaking for my child. But what happens when we send her to the nursery school where there are no men on the staff, where women are everywhere and do everything? What will she believe?" asked one father. "What will she grow up expecting of herself?"

Some feminist families have placed their young children in parent-cooperative nurseries, thinking at the beginning that the schools were what the name implied. "A parent cooperative means a mother cooperative," said one mother. Another mother had a similar experience. "Nick is in a cooperative nursery school where parents have to participate every couple of weeks. They went ahead and scheduled me without asking, assuming that I have every day free. They didn't go ahead and schedule any of the men. When I called up some of the parents to arrange a switch in schedules because they had me down for days that I teach, every time I got a man on the phone the same thing happened. 'Hello, I'm calling about changing times at the nursery school.' Every man said, 'Oh, you don't want me, that's my wife's department.' At the parent meeting nine men showed up out of seventy families. Rob went for us, because a friend was in the hospital. There was great praise and surprise that so many men showed. Damn, nine is a disgustingly low number. Those men should be involved."

"*Parents* must be involved in the schools. Those teachers must not say 'mother' all the time. Parent is the best term. It is not sex defined," charged a woman. "Sure some of the fathers work in the classroom, but not very many," reported another mother. "The teachers and children don't talk about the Helping Parent, they talk about the Helping Mama. They are reflecting the reality, but Helping Parent should be the umbrella phrase used. Will it make any difference that I'm one of the few that use the parent term? The idea of women in the classroom is so ingrained and hard to undo."

"We try so hard here at school to change a child's idea of sex roles. We set a good example, but if a child lives a sterotyped life at home, I'm pessimistic about what effects we have," commented one teacher.

All mothers and fathers want the best education for their children, but feminist parents have added some very specific ingredients to what they think makes up a quality education. "I don't care if it is open classroom or closed corridor, or what. That school better open up my children's heads about what is out there. I want them to choose what they want to do with their lives. I don't want it chosen for them," said a mother.

Feminist parents want the ideal. A progressive, well-equipped school, mixed ethnically, socio-economically, and sexually, preferably public and within walking distance even on a cold winter's day is a dream parents share. Such schools are not dotting the landscape. Mothers and fathers are settling for less.

But to the observer who has spent very little time in high schools or elementary schools for the last decade and a half, it looks like there is considerably more to settle for now. Schools are less menacing than they were, less formal. Take a look at the clothes, for example. School dress is looser for student and teacher.

Before pants became acceptable for decent women in the late sixties, all school girls wore dresses. Their clothes confined them as much as their sex roles did. Of course, little girls cried when they fell on the playground. Bare skin on macadam is painful. Of course, little girls ran away when the boys chased them. Only a masochist would join in a violent game when her knees would probably end up looking like raw hamburger.

Girls didn't run around the playground because they didn't want to fall and skin their bare knees. They didn't swing on the monkey bars because they were told nice little girls didn't let their panties show. They hated recess in winter because they suffered from the cold. The wind blew up their dresses and sometimes made them cry from the pain. For many women of that era biology was destiny, and wardrobe was destiny, too.

In the late forties, through the fifties, and well into the six-ties, only the more progressive schools encouraged children to come to class in work clothes. Elsewhere in this country, schools aspired to formality. Neatness was paramount. Private academies required the enforced neatness of uniforms. One parochial school in New Jersey mandated uniform shirts and jackets for the boys; for the girls, uniforms, white anklet socks, *and* seamless stockings. It was important their skin look smooth. Demerits were given for runs.

Any thought of fighting sex-role stereotyping was beyond comprehension. Girls looked and acted one way. Boys looked and acted another. The idea of attacking the eternal verities of the way boys and girls are, and how they should be, would have been looked on as heresy.

That was years ago, however. Today schools are addressing the issues of sexism and misogyny head-on. One high school staff member said, "The kids here are often addressed about sexism. I teach women's groups here. We talk about what is an okay male; what is an okay female. We try to get to the stereotypes and destroy them. We have the kids go out in the community, interview community members about sexism. We send the kids back to their own elementary school to observe how boys and girls are treated differently, or how they act differently. Of the twenty students I had in the last class, almost every one said, 'Yes, they are treated differently. Isn't that awful? I wouldn't do that to my kids.'"

"I teach a course to sophomores in the high school about human development," reported a teacher. "We start with early childhood and ask what qualities they think make a really good parent. What is the worst thing a parent could do to a child? I ask them to write descriptions of what is good and what is bad. I have them interview their parents. We share early school experiences, then I send the kids back to their own lower schools. They observe how girls are treated differently from boys. We talk about how distinctions based on sex are made. We talk about nursery rhymes. At the beginning of the year I come into the class and always find the boys over here, and all the girls over there. They divide themselves up. At fifteen, kids are off the wall a lot of the time. The boys are very immature in comparison to the girls."

"My course is called 'The Individual and Society' and deals with the kinds of institutions the individual has to deal with in development — like family, school, work. We talk about feminism and the traditional restraints on women. The kids in our school-within-a-school are really predisposed to feminism and the atmosphere is pretty loose. Very few teachers in the bigger high school go by their first names. One girl told me her parents won't let her call me Anne. 'Okay,' I said, 'Call me Ms.' I asked her if I should call her Ms. Johnson, but she said her first name was fine. I treat the kids as individuals and expect the same. But if her parents were forcing her to deal with a title, that's okay with me," said another high-school teacher.

"Our school committee decided that since we are a leadership system, we should address sex-role stereotyping in the schools," commented a high-school teacher. "The superintendent appointed a man to chair the committee! That man suggested I co-chair it with him. He thought a woman belonged at the head of the committee. We looked at physical education, at the general attitude in the schools towards women. We looked at the curriculum and materials and career aspirations. A lot of good things came out of it.

"We let publishing companies know we will no longer purchase sexist or biased materials. We collected a good set of slide shows and films addressing the questions of sexism. Now we need a corps of people who will take over and disseminate our findings. Right now, I get anything that comes in about sexism.

"Last year one group was planning a program on sex-role stereotyping. They asked me to help plan the program. I suggested the speakers. They sent an invitation to the superintendent of schools and to each top-level educator in the district. Every one of them sent their invitations to me! If a few of us are the repositories of all the sex-role information, what good is it?

"We've got to get the information out there, change the courses and change the society. Sure, the bright girls at the universities will still be motivated into careers, but they might never get into the really successful level in their careers unless we succeed in combating sex-role stereotyping. Otherwise, it is guaranteed frustration. Individual women will continue to make it by dint of their brilliance. But will there be a President of the United States who is a woman? A president of General Motors? There is not even a woman in the Senate!"

Many feminist families feel strongly that schools should be vocational training grounds that from the very beginning prepare a child to earn a living. Don't throw out liberal arts, just change the thrust of a liberal-arts education. Very few children will grow up to be princesses or princes. Only a very small number will be able to pay their bills by being a Renaissance woman or man. The job of the schools is to develop a child's aptitude, and to help her select a skill and translate that skill into income.

"Children must realize that they are going to be working, that they must do something with their lives," said one school librarian and parent. "Better they be committed to something very early. It may be entirely different by the time they grow up, but they should be interested in one career on another. The kids I see at our school are bored. It used to be they aspired to be cowboys, or something like that. Now, nothing."

"Our whole unit on careers is coming back to me now," said a mother of two elementary school-age sons. "All the kids in our elementary school class had to pick what we wanted to be and write away for materials from that industry. All the girls chose stewardess, model . . . I knew I couldn't be a model, I was too short . . . I eliminated that. Or they picked teacher, nurse, beautician, maybe two other things. If I had wanted to be an electrical engineer, first, I would have had to think of it. Second, I never would have had the nerve. Then we wrote away to something like the Suzy Downs Modeling School. There is no way I would have ever done a thing like write away to M.I.T.

"We all took the Kuder Preference Test. My occupation was supposed to be a fire ranger. It was the joke of the whole school. In 1961, it was so funny. It was like a mistake.

"We never had to follow up that career unit. We wrote away, got the pamphlets, and that was it."

It is important to let little girls and boys know they can be anything, and it is imperative to show them women and men who do a variety of jobs. "We make a special point of showing all the children the jobs in the community. Sewing is something a tailor does to make a living. It is not just something your mother does to your shirt buttons," explains a nursery-school teacher.

"For the little children we try to bring workers of all types into the classroom. A female and male chef came to visit. We cooked eggs and talked about cooking in restaurants, in luncheonettes, and in diners. I think they have more respect for the meal preparation their parents do. Very little children know that something is more valuable if you are paid for it. They met people in the classroom that are paid to cook," offered another nursery-school teacher,

"This work unit has taken a lot of work. We've had to find workers in non-stereotyped jobs, then schedule field trips to a bakery, a lumberyard.

"Our trip to a law firm was a bust. Sure there were women

and men lawyers, but the place was a bore. To a young child an office is an office. In fact, the typing pool looks like a lot more fun than a lawyer's private office. They don't care if a desk is rosewood, or plastic laminate. Office work looks dull."

A number of teachers reported they decorate their classrooms with pictures of women and men in non-stereotyped jobs. "We used the set called 'People at Work' distributed by the Women's Action Alliance," said a play-group leader. If the living and breathing proof that people can perform in non-stereotyped jobs is not available in your community, proof in pictures is available by mail. "Whenever I see a picture of someone at work that I think would expand the kids' horizons I cut it out and bring it to school. The advertisers may try to sell me their products by printing a picture of a woman doctor, well I'll cut off their advertising copy and try to sell my ideas with the help of their picture," said a teacher.

Another job of the schools is to educate children about the nature of work both inside and outside the home. A number of day-care center and nursery schools conduct units on home work, or household management. When a child says the mother doesn't work, the image of a television-watching bonbon eater may flash across your mind. The child neglects to mention the two babies at home who create a lot of work.

"I was very impressed with the unit they did on work at the day-care center. One of the other parents told me our daughter said her father worked in an office and at home, and that I worked at home nursing and taking care of her new brother," said a proud mother. "She's growing up with a healthy respect for women's work, be it child tending or making money. She sees me do both."

By kindergarten age children have a clear impression of what jobs are suitable for men and what jobs are suitable for women. In *Undoing Sex Stereotypes,* Marcia Guttentag and Helen Bray report the results of a six-week intervention in three school systems where they tried to attack sex-role stereotyping. Asking kindergartners to make lists of jobs, both girls and boys listed significantly more jobs for men than for women. Although they reported mostly lower-status jobs for men — the work they saw performed daily — children of both sexes felt men had more options. The work listed for women was highly stereotyped: housecleaner, nurse, teacher.

After the six-week program, in which great attention was paid to increasing the children's awareness of jobs both women and men could hold, the kindergartners' attitudes and lists changed. There was no longer any clear differentiation between male and female jobs. Stereotyped jobs for women were joined by very unstereotyped jobs for females. The chance of women holding high-status jobs was easily absorbed by the kindergarten girls.

Dreams of glory and high pay are quite standard among elementary-school girls. It is usually during adolescence, when a girl reaches high school and she should be charting how to make her dream a reality, that girls give up. In her early teens a girl may decide it is more important to have a date Saturday night than to study and do well on a physics test. Social pressure on teen-age girls is greater than academic or career pressure.

"When the world has changed enough to accept little girls who do not hang back and hide their intellect," suggests one psychiatrist, "when making a good catch of a man is not all that is expected, it will be easier. Until then it takes strong, courageous parents to give a child enough support so she will feel comfortable enough to buck the norm."

Girls who "buck the norm" between the ages of ten and fourteen, as well as boys who reject the pressures to join the pack, succeed to a greater extent in later life.

One high school guidance counselor claims that "some of us are ranting and raving about the way girls seem to give up on some subjects once they are in high school, but I fear it's a voice in a wind storm."

Parents and teachers alike are showing and telling high schoolers that it is much easier to be a secretary or file clerk, after you've prepared to be a biochemist, than the other way around.

"Every kid in our school has sessions in the career center," reports a high-school guidance counselor. "We talk about negative choices made for careers. We talk about doors that slam shut if you don't prepare. We have no way to tell what effect it has on the girls, although we are hopeful. We do go out of our way to eliminate sexist books and sexist directions that girls and boys are given. We make sure we react the same when a boy or girl comes into the guidance office and says she or he wants to drop math.

"We get materials from the society of women engineers. We try very hard to get minority examples of professions in here. Last year, for example, I had a black female dentist visit."

Girls are expected to flounder in math and the sciences. "It starts in preschool. Girls and boys are taught numbers and math by women teachers who never resolved their own blocks with the subject. They introduce mathematics never fully expecting the girls to excel. Subliminally girls are told to remove themselves from mathematical territory. By the time they get to junior high and the male teachers that teach math and science, the girls have already given up. If women teachers can't do math well, or more importantly, if they can't do it comfortably, how can we expect small girls to?" complained a grown-up woman who today has trouble balancing her checkbook.

Wesleyan and Wellesley are among the colleges that have math-anxiety clinics to tutor young women through the mathematical morass. If a woman didn't do well in the advanced high-school math and science classes, there is little hope she will pick up college-level courses and succeed. The clinics help women shore up both their confidence and lack of experience in those fields.

At least one high school has adopted the same tutorial approach for girls interested in courses traditionally attracting mostly boys. Says one administrator-teacher, "A math teacher here at the high school teaches a very high-level math course. Last year only five girls completed the course, a very small number. She decided to form a support system for those girls to encourage them to stick with it — to take the fear away and to help them do it. This year the class is huge. The preponderance is girls!

"At the senior level, girls in advanced-placement in physics and math are rare. The girls in the AP-math and AP-physics are rare. It is a ratio of seven or eight boys to one girl. The assistant superintendent wants to form support systems for girls in all areas of difficulty.

"I tell the kids, particularly the girls, to try anything. To prepare themselves for careers. If I had my doctorate, I'd have a better chance of doing the work I would like — being a principal. But I do not have the doctorate or the kind of experience they are requiring for the job I know I could do. I don't want to spend three years getting a doctorate. We have two in college, two more coming right up.

"I regret not knowing at thirty-two, instead of forty-two, that there is a direction I want to go in. I value the nurturing I did for the kids, but I didn't have to do it full time. I don't regret the time I spent with the kids, but I do regret that there was a whole lag in my life that I can never make up. It is not recoverable."

The percentage of women entering law school and medical school is now around 25 percent. Dentistry and veterinary science are still low. "Careers in the professions for women are on the rise," says Boston psychiatrist Carol Nadelson. "Women are entering medicine in increasing numbers. Currently 20 percent of the students are women. In four years the percentage will go up. At Harvard, right now, a third in the class are women. But what are they going to do professionally? No one is planning. What do you do if you are a surgical resident and you are having a baby? If you don't change the system that requires long shifts in the hospital and little sleep, how are you going to deal with it? It is not do-able. If you have a little baby? If you have a man who will share half? Who works half or part time? You don't find professional men doing that. Our culture doesn't support it. We hear more now from the men and women medical students about how they are feeling. But, for professional women, the numbers don't look as good as they should by now."

The only way feminist parents are ever going to help those numbers improve is to force schools to offer quality non-sexist education. According to Marcia Guttentag's investigation into sex-role stereotyping, the most important factor that determines the effectiveness of a non-sexist childraising program is the classroom teacher. An enthusiastic, skilled, fair-minded teacher translates the ideas of open horizons for both sexes into realities.

Research by psychologists and sociologists shows that it is difficult to find such teachers, since most teachers do treat different sex children unequally and prefer children of the opposite sex. Studies conducted by Dr. Lisa Serbin, a psychologist at the State University of New York at Binghamton, showed that boys get more attention than girls. Reporting her findings to the Women's Action Alliance Conference on Early Childhood Education, Serbin claimed that boys received from teachers eight times more detailed instruction than girls. Teachers took boys step by step and taught them how to solve problems. Boys were both praised and punished more frequently. When a boy child threatened another child in the classroom, Serbin's observations show the teacher intervened 75 percent of the time, but intervened when a girl child threatened only 25 percent of the time.

Serbin notes some factors that can make the classroom experience a negative one for girls. Teachers paid more attention to boys when they were close by and when they were far away in the classroom. Girls, however, got two to three times more attention from the teacher only when they were close by. When they drifted out of a teacher's immediate proximity, it was as if they disappeared. In effect, the independent girl who moves away from the teacher may well be ignored. When she gets stuck in a difficult project, the teacher will not discern her predicament as quickly as if she were a boy. The girl may be left frustrated. If she is noticed, the girl will most probably have the problem solved for her by the teacher, or told not to try something as difficult.

Fortunately there are teachers who are exceptions to the rule. There are extraordinary teachers who are combating sexism in the classroom and in themselves. They continue to raise their own consciousnesses, change their behavior, and change their classrooms. With higher consciousnesses about sexism, children can then move out from under the guidance of a non-sexist teacher and into the class of a sexist teacher without backsliding. "There are some teachers in the lower schools in town who have raised the kids' consciousnesses at a young age," said a high-school teacher. "As a result, if a math teacher, for example, makes a sexist comment in class the kids call him on it. They don't let it go. Later I'll hear them talking about it, or they'll tell me, 'You wouldn't believe what he said!' "

"Teachers have made a big difference in our school district. They've been young and progressive and established a very liberal curriculum. We've had a Women and Society course in our high school for six years," boasted a teacher and parent. But even in classrooms of aware teachers there are slips on the non-sexist front. "My son is very tuned in. So apparently are the kids in his class," reported a parent. "A little girl in the class asked the teacher, 'Why do you ask the boys to move the blackboard? I can do it.' The teacher had not realized what she was doing. At six they are all tiny. The boys are no bigger or stronger than the girls," "I feel good when the kids correct me," said a teacher. "It means they've processed the idea of sexism and taken it to the next level. It means I've taught them well."

"I try to catch myself. I try to say 'children' instead of boys and girls," said another teacher. "We always had the girls get their coats in a group, then the boys. Now I have one side of the room get up first, or I ask all the children wearing one color to work as a unit. The assumption that children are alike because they are the same sex is wrong. A boy and a girl may have tons more in common than two boys." One preschool teacher puts girls and boys together because of her politics and because of her own school experience. "We try to mix girls and boys as much as possible, because that is the way the world is. I went to a girls' school and I learned that boys were something different from me. I don't think that was a good lesson. I want the children to learn truths and realities they can apply to the rest of their lives."

Schools will continue to be sexist until there is a commitment to fighting sexism on the same level as the commitment to fight illiteracy. Education is an anti-illiteracy campaign; it should be an anti-sexism campaign as well. Although there are devoted individuals in the schools who are fighting sexism, they are few in number. We cannot just wait for the schools to change from within. Involved parents must pressure from without to make a difference.

Barbara Grizzuti Harrison wrote *Unlearning The Lie* about fighting sexism at her children's private school in Brooklyn. As part of a sex-roles committee, Harrison carefully examined the school environment for sexism. The committee found it and took arms against it.

The sex-roles committee held a joint parent-staff meeting and a videotape, prepared by the committee, was shown which illustrated how the media depicts women and girls in demeaning ways. A paper by psychologists on the difference in the modes of cognition and perception in girls and boys was read, along with a paper on the image of women in literature. The committee also offered a symposium on women in history. That evening's presentation began a chain of events that brought sexism into focus and succeeded in diluting sexism at the school.

Schools do respond to parent pressure. Especially at private schools, a twenty- or thirty-family group could have clout in this time of a declining birthrate. Add up the number of children in a family group that big; then multiply the number of children by the tuition. You will have a reading of the group's power in dollars and cents. If it comes down to it, a sex-roles committee could threaten to withdraw its children and money if a non-sexist program is not adopted. Appealing to a school's sense of fairness and justice is of course the preferred first course of action

Public-school parents do have the option of withholding the school tax, but that course of action shouldn't be the first, either. Public school parents can use the political process to elect feminists to the school boards. However, the most effective change happens after you come at the schools from all sides.

Become a presence in the classroom. Talk with the teacher about sexism either individually, as a group, or both. Observe during school hours. Are children treated as individuals, or are they treated differently according to sex? An excellent questionnaire-checklist was developed by Felicia George, Assistant Project Director of the Women's Action Alliance Non-Sexist Child Development Project, and it can be obtained by writing to the Alliance. It is meant to be used as a self-evaluating tool for teachers, but it can be adopted by parents as a tool to judge your children's classrooms. It will check out your own hidden sexism, as well. Take it into the classroom, look, listen, and record your answers.

You might ask the teachers in the school to take the checklist and record their own responses, too. Then at a staff meeting, or at a parent-staff meeting, the result of the checklist could be discussed. Ways to combat hidden sexism might be suggested.

Examine the books in the classrooms. Take along the how-to-spot-sexism checklist in the "Books Can Be Friends" chapter of this book. Are there quality books about girls on the bookshelves? What readers are used? Do the teachers point out sexism when and if it appears?

Barbara Sprung, Director of the Non-sexist Child Development Project for The Women's Action Alliance, has written *Non-Sexist Education for Young Children: A Practical Guide*. The book offers fine suggestions how to purge a classroom of sexism. It would be an excellent springboard for the discussion of sexism in the classroom for teachers alone, or parents and teachers together.

Sprung's book is the result of the first model project conducted by the Women's Action Alliance, which is a non-profit, educational organization, established in 1971. The Alliance states that its purpose is "to help translate a growing awareness of sex discrimination into concrete actions and improvements in the lives of women. The Alliance offers information, research resources, model projects, a referral system, and other tools through which women of all economic and ethnic groups can work for both personal and institutional change."

Barbara Sprung and her crew studied sexist influences and actions in day-care centers in the New York metropolitan area, then worked with four volunteer demonstration centers to test non-sexist materials and programs for young children. Five study units on Families, Jobs People Do, The Human Body, Homemaking, and Sports were field tested in the demonstration centers and are applicable to almost any preschool classroom.

In October 1976, the Women's Action Alliance held a conference on non-sexist early childhood education for 250 early childhood educators. For three days, the Alliance presented addresses, workshops, discussions, and films that ran the gamut of the issue of sexism, children, and education. There was an overview of the research into sex roles in schools and a discussion of androgyny. There were how-to-implement-a-non-sexist-curriculum workshops; discussions of how to confront the male sex-role stereotype, how to educate parents, and so on. The Alliance marshaled a massive assault on sexism in early childhood education that bodes well for our children.

Sadly, the pure non-sexist thrust of the conference was blunted from the outset by participants who argued that racism is more important than sexism. It was as if the brown and black women feared there isn't enough energy to fight sexism and racism simultaneously. It was as if the brown and black women were saying to the white, while you are hollering about getting your daughters into architectural school, we are yelling about getting decent food into our daughters. The argument was classism and privilege, not sexism or racism.

To white women at the conference the legitimacy of the feminist complaint was at issue. Do we as second-class citizens of the majority race have a right to give our already relatively privileged children more chances? Is the fight against sexism a white-middle-class women's battle? Letty Cottin Pogrebin, a *Ms.* Magazine editor, author, and feminist lecturer, spoke angrily and eloquently that misogyny cuts across all race lines. No matter how much the men of color suffer, the women of color suffer more. Racism and sexism are a heavy double burden to bear; they are both antithetical to full human growth. They must both be fought at the same time. One way to fight is through education.

14

VISIONS

WHERE are we in the project of raising non-sexist children? Clearly, some children are on their way to living non-sexist lives, but nowhere near the number there would be if combating sexism were a national or international goal. Yet considering the ineffectiveness of the 1960s national war on poverty, marshaling a country-wide assault on sexism might enshrine female suppression instead of eliminating it. I do fantasize how Madison Avenue, not Washington, could fight sexism. Any industry that can sell talking margarine could undoubtedly persuade countless numbers of people to buy non-sexism.

Without a Madison Avenue campaign, without an ERA, I am forced to entertain dreams of being a benevolent dictator for the sexist masses. Part of my dictatorial powers would be to appoint a screening board with power to remove sexist material from newspapers, magazines, television, movies, books — all of course in clear violation of the Constitution. We would rewrite the dictionary and retune our ears to hear a non-sexist language. Sex prejudice in its blatant and subtle forms would be out. Fair-minded thinking would be in. I would hasten a slow progress by flaunting the tenets of a democracy if I didn't know it would be dangerous and immoral. I am impatient with the system. I want it to be fairer, faster.

I have a vision of the children I would like to raise. Twins — a girl and a boy — who would be dressed like children, not identifiably the female and male of the species. They would be given the best of materials and toys. Their personalities would develop free of sex-related restrictions or directions. They each would be free to be whatever and whoever and however they choose. They would be happy, of course. Fulfill their potential, of course. And be a pleasure and pride to a fair-thinking world.

But, in all fairness, I ask myself if I really mean what I say. Am I liberated enough to allow the freedom I say I want? Am I liberated enough to understand it if my daughter chooses to be a business tycoon, or a Roman Catholic priest? Will I be pleased if my son stays home full time until his youngest child is in school? If my children are free to choose, and they choose not to have children of their own, can I respect their choice? If they fall into stereotypic roles, do I blame myself for failing to counteract the forces of a male-biased society? I wonder if they would reject my militancy because it is "mother's," and with it reject fairness?

The non-sexist dream is sometimes a personal nightmare.

If we really are to free ourselves to raise nonsexist children, we must come to terms with our own upbringings. Vicki Britebart, the mother of a girl and a boy, admits that many times when she and her husband share the parenting, "We are the ones who feel like the oddballs, not the kids. What we are doing goes against our training."

What was that training? Twenty and thirty years ago there were rather strict lessons about what it is to be a man or a woman. Even if our families deviated ever so slightly from the norm, we learned from television, movies, storybooks, readers at school, and from everyone in positions of power in our society exactly what a man and woman *should* be. There were few doubts.

The children of the Vicki and Eric Britebarts — children who are raised in a family where participatory parenthood and a non-sexist attitude are the norm — will not feel like "oddballs," however; they are not being taught that mamas do this and papas do that. Those of us grownups who were trained to believe that the sexes have very different jobs — she: dishes, he: garbage — can't help but feel like "oddballs" sometimes. Our conditioning is too strong. While we may be able to deprogram our heads, we are not able to deprogram our guts.

My own stomach churns as I fight against my conditioning, to be a different kind of parent, a new kind of mother. As I write this, my three-year-old daughter is with another child and a babysitter at the home of a friend. Casey didn't want to go there — she has had four consecutive mornings and afternoons of babysitters and not enough mama. This morning she climbed into her bed, pulled up the quilt and announced, "I can stay here with you if I take a nap."

Her crying and wanting me gets me in my gut — that part of me that was taught to believe that mamas should always be there. So I spent extra time talking and snuggling and planning the playing we will do later. I am resolved about the kind of parenting I want to do, so I did take her to the babysitter and returned to work. But I am still torn by her pain and by my own conditioning.

It is of paramount importance to me that I set a good example of what a woman is — someone committed to work and ideals in addition to child, husband, and home. But at the same time my training tells me that my child should come first, that my primary job as a mother is to serve my child while she is young. I and so many other feminist mothers I have talked with need to remind ourselves that the conditioning is wrong.

How different is the training today's fathers must undergo. They not only have to undo the training that has told them children are women's work, not manly enough for them, but they have to learn the parenting skills without years of practice. My husband and other feminist fathers like him did not nurture baby dolls when they were growing up. Slowly, haltingly, and sometimes fearfully, they have developed a feeling of competence in caring for children. They have had to battle the gnawing feeling that "men don't do this" — the bottle feeding, diaper changing, laundry sorting, room straightening, peanut butter sandwich making, as well as the myriad maintenance chores that make up parenting.

Feminist parents must undertake on-the-job retraining.

They must teach themselves and their children at the same time what is acceptable behavior for both sexes. They must make our society realize that female children's liberation is male children's liberation, too.

Raising a non-sexist child in a sexist world is a lonely and difficult job. There are no precedents, no kind of program that we know will pay off in allowing our children to grow up free of the restrictions the world will try to place on them because of gender. The job requires extraordinary patience and perseverance. We have a long, hard, and frustrating road ahead. Once sex discrimination is illegal, with the passage of the Equal Rights Amendment and anti-sexist legislation, then feminists will be on better ground to attack the discriminatory and derogatory practices of our culture. The gap between equal standing under the law and equal treatment is immense, however. Sexism cannot be legislated out of existence.

What then is the answer?

Since boy children are preferred to girl children in most of our society, it surely would advance the cause of non-sexist childraising if we muted the differences between the sexes from the very beginning. Let's treat all babies as babies, not as boys or girls. If all infants in hospital nurseries were wrapped in yellow blankets, instead of pink and blue, and labeled on a neutral color card BABY SMITH-JONES, instead of BABY GIRL, or BABY BOY, maybe all infants would be treated as equally terrific. Then, as in Lois Gould's story about the child named X, if the identifying genitalia were hidden, both sexes would be treated as Preferred — instead of one Preferred, the other Class B.

With that suggestion I am inviting the wrath of feminists, female chauvinists, and thinkers of many persuasions. Why then suggest homogenization for the women-children's movement? Only because we need a temporary measure to use until our society comes to value the two sexes equally. Unitl that time, during the period of adjustment, let's stop talking about raising girls and boys and speak instead of raising children.

RESOURCES

The following organizations offer a wide variety of resources and materials for non-sexist childraising:

Action for Children's Television (ACT), 46 Austin Street, Newtonville, Massachusetts 02160, offers guidelines on television watching.

American Society for Psychoprophylaxis in Obstetrics (ASPO). Local chapters are widespread; the national headquarters is ASPO, 1523 L Street, NW, Washington, D.C. 20005.

Alternate birth centers are accessible through your local hospital association. Here are some individual centers: Mount Zion Hospital, San Francisco; the Mendocino Coast Hospital, Fort Bragg, California; the Maternity Center Association (also called the MCA Childbearing Center), 48 East 92nd Street, New York City; the Booth Maternity Center, Philadelphia; The New Life Center Family Hospital, Milwaukee.

American Federation of Teachers, The Women's Rights Committee, 1012 Fourteenth Street, NW, Washington, D.C. 20005.

American Library Association, 4004 Whitman North, Seattle, Washington 98104, has a Task Force on the Status of Women.

Change for Children, 2588 Mission Street, Room 226, San Francisco, California 94110, has an educational action project to fight sex role and racial stereotyping.

Children's Book Council, 175 Fifth Avenue, New York, New York 10010, offers information on publishing children's books. If you have a non-sexist ms. up your sleeve, send a stamped, self-addressed envelope above.

Council on Interracial Books for Children, 1841 Broadway, New York, New York 10023, promotes anti-sexist and anti-racist literature and instructional material for children.

Feminist Book Mart, 162-11 Ninth Avenue, Whitestone, New York, offers a catalog of its children's and adult's books. *Little Miss Muffet . . .* is available here for $1.00.

Feminist Press, P.O. Box 224, Old Westbury, New York 11568, publishes books for children and non-sexist material for elementary schools.

Feminists on Children's Media compiled *Little Miss Muffet Fights Back* and wrote "Feminist Look at Children's Books," *School Library Journal*, January 1971, pp. 19–24, which looks at some highly touted stories for school children.

KNOW, Inc., P.O. Box 86031, Pittsburgh, Pennsylvania, 15221, publishes divers articles on the feminist movement.

Lollipop Power, P.O. Box 1171, Chapel Hill, North Carolina 27514, specializes in early childhood books.

MS Magazine, 370 Lexington Avenue, New York, New York 10017, offers "Stories for Free Children" and columns on non-sexist books.

National Education Association, 1201 Sixteenth Street, Washington, D.C. 20036, reprints articles on sexism in education.

National Institute of Education, The Office of Education, 400 Maryland Avenue, SW, Washington, D.C. 20202.

National Organization for Women (NOW), Public Information Office, 527 Madison Avenue, Suite 1001, New York, New York 10002.

Public Action Coalition on Toys (PACT), 38 W. 9th Street, New York, New York 10011, is a consumer watchdog group that wants to make playthings more responsive to children's needs. PACT presents annual awards to toy makers as positive reinforcement for non-sexist, non-racist, non-violent toys. PACT offers a how-to-choose-toys guideline.

Racism/Sexism Resource Center, Room 300, 1941 Broadway, New York, New York 10023, offers a free catalog listing student and teacher materials for women's study classes and for human relations training. The center also offers documented statistics on sexism.

Resource Center on Sex Roles in Education, 1156 Fifteenth Street, Washington, D.C. 20005.

Sex Equality in Guidance Opportunities, 1607 New Hampshire Avenue, NW, Washington, D.C. 20009.

Womanbooks, 201 West 92nd Street, New York, New York 10025, a comprehensive bookstore devoted to feminism, children, children's books, childbirth, and you-name-it.

Women's Action Alliance, 370 Lexington Avenue, New York, New York 10017, offers non-sexist curricular material, as well as their line of non-sexist toys.

Women's Equity Action League, National Press Building, Washington, D.C. 20045, offers legislation, legislative action, and information.

Women on Words and Images, P.O. Box 2163, Princeton, New Jersey 08540, rents out a slide show and sells a pamphlet entitled "Dick and Jane as Victims," which documents sexism in children's school readers. They also offer a study on sexism in children's television, "Channeling Children: Sex Stereotyping in Prime Time TV."

BIBLIOGRAPHY

Ames, Elinor, "Would You Hire a Boy as Your Child's Sitter?" *New York Sunday News,* June 6, 1976.

Bene, E., "On the Genesis of Female Homosexuality," *British Journal of Psychiatry* 111 (1965): 815–821.

Beyers, Charlotte K., "The Best Way to Have a Baby," *Parents Magazine,* August 1976.

"Child Care Data and Materials," *U.S. Department of Labor 1975 Handbook on Women Workers,* October 1974.

DeMause, Lloyd, "The Evolution of Childhood," in Lloyd DeMause, ed., *The History of Childhood* (New York: Harper & Row, 1974).

Ellis, Albert, and Robert A. Harper, *A New Guide to Rational Living* (Englewood Cliffs, N.J.: Prentice-Hall, 1975).

Erikson, Erik H., *Identity: Youth and Crisis* (New York: W.W. Norton, 1968).

Farrell, Warren, *The Liberated Man — Beyond Masculinity: Freeing Men and Their Relationships with Women* (New York: Random House, 1974).

Fasteau, Marc Feigen, *The Male Machine* (New York: McGraw-Hill, 1974).

Gilder, George F., *Sexual Suicide,* (New York: Quadrangle Books, 1973).

Gould, Lois, "X: A Fabulous Child's Story," in Maggie Tripp, ed., *Woman in the Year 2000* (New York: Arbor House, 1974).

Guttentag, Marcia, and Helen Bray, *Undoing Sex Stereotypes: A Resource Book for Teachers* (New York: McGraw-Hill, 1976).

Harrison, Barbara Grizzutti, *Unlearning the Lie: Sexism in School* (New York: Liveright, 1973).

Hochstein, Rollie, "Today's Daughter, Tomorrow's Woman," *Family Circle,* November 1975.

Jespersen, Otto, *The Growth and Structure of the English Language* (New York; The Free Press, 1968).

Kaye, H. E., "Lesbian Relationships," *Sexual Behavior,* April 1971, pp. 80–87.

Maccoby, Eleanor Emmons, and Carol Nagy Jacklin, *The Psychology of Sex Differences* (Stanford: Stanford University Press, 1974).

Perez, Cecilia, Bonni R. Seegmiller, and Dorothy Ranier, "Sex Role Stereotyping in Television Commercials" (unpublished study, 1976).

Racism/Sexism Resource Center, "Fact Sheets on Institutional Sexism," March 1976.

Rich, Adrienne, *Of Woman Born: Motherhood as Experience and Institution* (New York, W.W. Norton, 1976).

Rivers, Caryl, "Can a Woman Be Liberated and Married?" *The New York Times Magazine,* November 2, 1975.

Rosen, David, *Lesbianism: The Multiple Roots of Homosexuality* (New York: Basic Books, 1975).

Serbin, Lisa, "Teachers, Peers and Play Preferences: An Environmental Approach to Sex Typing in the Preschool" (paper presented to the Conference on Early Childhood Education, sponsored by the Women's Action Alliance, in October 1976).

Sexton, Patricia Cayo, *The Feminized Male: Classrooms, White Collars, and the Decline of Manliness* (New York: Random House, 1969).

Sheehy, Gail, *Passages* (New York: E. P. Dutton, 1976).

Singer, June, *Androgyny: Toward a New Theory of Sexuality* (New York: Doubleday, 1976).

Sprung, Barbara, *Non-Sexist Education for Young Children: A Practical Guide* (New York: Scholastic Book Services, 1975).

Tanzer, Deborah, and Jean Libman Block, *Why Natural Childbirth?: A Psychologist's Report on the Benefits to Mothers, Fathers, and Babies* (New York: Doubleday, 1972).

Van Gelder, Lindsy, and Carrie Carmichael, "But What About Our Sons?" *Ms.* (October 1975).

ABOUT THE AUTHOR

Carrie Carmichael is heard daily on "Workplace," a new program on the NBC radio network. She is associate producer and host of a weekly women's interest television program in New York City, and was associate producer for a documentary about the First National Women's Conference, "After Houston, What Next?" She has been an actress and singer, and is the author of two children's books, *Bigfoot: Man, Myth, or Monster*, and *Secrets of the Great Magicians*.

An article, "But What About Our Sons," written with Lindsy Van Gelder for *Ms.* magazine, was the basis for *Non-Sexist Childraising*.

Carmichael lives in Manhattan with her husband, Jeff Greenfield, and daughter Casey.